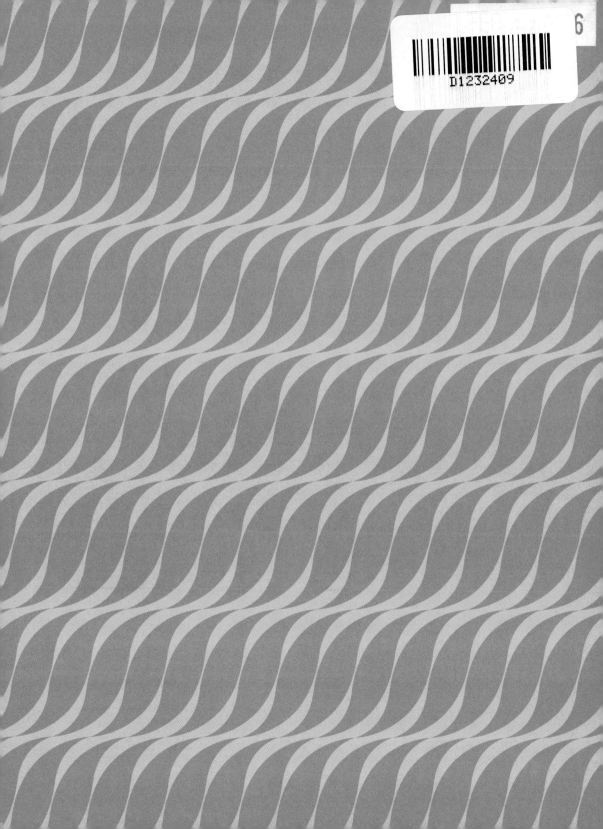

FIND OUT ABOUT

MESOPOTAMIA

*What life was like in ancient Sumer,
Babylon and Assyria*

Lorna Oakes

CONSULTANT – Dr. John Haywood

southwater

For my grandson Charlie Bridgeman

This edition is published by Southwater

Southwater is an imprint of Anness Publishing Ltd
Hermes House, 88–89 Blackfriars Road, London SE1 8HA
tel. 020 7401 2077; fax 020 7633 9499
www.southwaterbooks.com; info@anness.com

© Anness Publishing Ltd 2001, 2003

UK agent: The Manning Partnership Ltd,
tel. 01225 478 444; fax 01225 478 440;
sales@manning-partnership.co.uk

UK distributor: Grantham Book Services Ltd
tel. 01476 541080; fax 01476 541061;
orders@gbs.tbs-ltd.co.uk

North American agent/distributor: National Book Network,
tel. 301 459 3366; fax 301 429 5746; www.nbnbooks.com

Australian agent/distributor: Pan Macmillan Australia,
tel. 1300 135 113; fax 1300 135 103;
customer.service@macmillan.com.au

Publisher: Joanna Lorenz
Managing Editor, Children's Books: Gilly Cameron Cooper
Project Editor: Joy Wotton
Editor: Nicola Baxter
Editorial Reader: Penelope Goodare
Designer: Margaret Sadler
Illustration: Rob Ashby, Vanessa Card,
Rob Sheffield, Clive Spong
Picture Research: Carrie Haines, Sarah Hopper
Project Photography: John Freeman
Stylist: Melanie Williams
Production Controller: Yolande Denny

Anness Publishing would like to thank Scallywags and the
following children for modeling for this book: Mikey Ammah,
Earaneqa Carter, Stephanie Da Cova, Gem Harrison, Lorenzo
Heron, Eka Karumidze, Louis Loucaides, Alex Martin-Simons,
Ernests Milevics, Kayleigh Ollman, Gigi Playfair, Dimitry
Rozamae, Victoria Sintun, Luke Spencer and Nino Zaalishvili.

PICTURE CREDITS
b=bottom, t=top, c=center, m=middle, l=left, r=right
AKG: 2bl, 3br, 4tl, 8tl, 9mr, 10tl, 14t, 16t, 18t, 19tl, 22bc,
24tl, 24mc, 26b, 27tl, 28ml, 28mr, 29tl, 30tr, 34tl, 36t, 37tr,
40t, 41ml, 43bl, 44t, 45tl, 47m, 49tr, 53tr, 58b, 59tr, 59br,
61tr; Ancient Art and Architecture Collection: 54t, 54br, 60t;
Bildarchiv Preussischer Kulturbesitz: 3tr, 9tr, 11bl, 14bl, 14br,
15ml, 17t, 17bl, 19tr, 26t, 27br, 29m, 33ml, 41tl, 42t, 42ml,
48b, 52tl, 54bl, 60b; Bulloz: 11br, 12tl, 26m, 29tr, 42mr; Mary
Evans Picture Library: 13me.t. archive, 45b, 61b; Werner
Forman: 20t; Robert Harding Picture Library: 5t, 19ml, 20mr,
21ml, 21mc, 27tr, 31tr, 31t, 33tr, 36b, 44br, 50t, 52mr, 53ml,
55br, 57tl, 59tl; David Hawkins: 11t, 38b; Michael Holford:
5mr, 8tr, 9rl, 16bl, 20ml, 22t, 22ml, 23tl, 31bl, 34ml, 43t,
50mr, 56t, 58t; Hutchison Library: 22br, 30br; Ident: 18m;
Erich Lessing: 55tl; John Oakes: 23bl, 37bl; Muriel and
Giovanni Dagli Orti: 12mr, 30ml, 46t; Science and Society
Picture Library: 56ml

Previously published as *Step into Mesopotamia*

10 9 8 7 6 5 4 3 2 1

CONTENTS

A Land Between Two Rivers

MESOPOTAMIA is the name of an ancient region where some of the world's first cities and empires grew up. Today, most of it lies in modern Iraq. Mesopotamia means 'the land between the rivers'—for the country lay between the Tigris and the Euphrates, two mighty rivers that flowed from the highlands of Turkey in the north down to the Gulf.

The first farmers settled in the low, rolling hills of the north about 9,000 years ago. Here, there was enough rainfall to grow crops and provide pasture for animals. The first cities developed about 3,500 years later, mostly in the flat, fertile flood plains of the south. Rivers and marshes provided water to irrigate crops, plenty of fish, and reeds to build houses and boats. Date palms grew in abundance. At first the south was called Sumer. Later it was known as Babylonia. The land in north Mesopotamia became known as Assyria.

SUMERIAN WORSHIPERS

Statues of a man and woman from Sumer are shown in an act of worship. The Sumerians were some of the earliest people to live in the south of Mesopotamia. They lived in small, independent cities. At the center of each city was a temple built as the home for the local god. These two Sumerians had statues made of themselves and put in a temple so that the god could bless them.

THE WORK OF GIANTS

Most of what we know about the ancient civilizations of Mesopotamia has come from excavations by archaeologists over the last 150 years. In 1845, the British archaeologist Henry Layard unearthed the remains of a once-magnificent palace in the ancient Assyrian city of Nimrud. He found walls decorated with scenes of battles and hunting, and a statue of a human-headed, winged lion so huge that local people were astonished and thought it had been made by giants.

TIMELINE 7000–2100 B.C.

Humans have lived in northern Iraq since the Old Stone Age, when hunter-gatherers lived in caves and rock shelters and made stone tools. Mesopotamian civilization began when people began to settle in villages. They learned how to grow crops and keep animals. Later, city-states grew up, and people developed writing. They became good at building, working metal and making fine jewelry.

painted pottery

7000 B.C. The first villages are established. Edible plants and animals are domesticated, and farming develops. Pottery is made and mud-bricks used for building.

6000 B.C. Use of copper. First mural paintings, temples and seals. Irrigation is used in agriculture to bring water to the fields. Decorated pottery, clay and alabaster figurines. Wide use of brick.

clay figurine

4000 B.C. Larger houses and temples are built. Terra-cotta sickles and pestles are developed.

3500 B.C. Growth of towns. Development of the potter's wheel, the plow, the first cylinder seals and writing. Bronze, silver and gold worked. Sculptures are made. Trading systems develop.

writing tablet

3000 B.C. Sumerian civilization begins. City-states and writing develop.

7000 B.C.   4000 B.C.   2700 B.C.

TEMPLES OF THE GODS

The ziggurat of Nanna, the Moon god, rises above the dusty plains of modern Iraq. It was once part of the massive temple complex in the city of Ur. Ziggurats showed how clever the Mesopotamians were at building. They were designed as a link between heaven and earth.

WRITING TABLET

A clay tablet shows an example of some of the earliest writing in the world. The symbols were pressed into a damp clay tablet using a reed pen. The Sumerians originally used writing to keep accounts of goods bought and sold including grain and cattle. Later on, kings used clay tablets as a record of their victories and building activities. Scribes wrote letters, poems and stories about heroes.

POWERFUL NEIGHBORS

The kingdom of Egypt lay to the southwest of Mesopotamia. In about 2000 B.C. the Assyrians traded with Anatolia in the northwest. They later conquered Phoenician cities in the west and fought Urartu in the north.

Sumerian chariot

2700 B.C. Early Dynastic period. Kings and city administrations rule.

2600 B.C. Royal Standard of Ur made, probably as the sounding box of a lyre.

2500 B.C. Royal Graves of Ur made. Queen Pu-abi and other wealthy individuals buried in tombs with soldiers, musicians and court ladies.

2440 B.C. Interstate warfare. Kings of Lagash go to war with Umma.

2334 B.C. Sargon of Agade becomes king. He creates the world's first empire, which is maintained by his grandson Naram-sin.

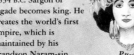

Pu-abi

2200 B.C. The Agade Empire comes to an end. The Gutians, a mountain people, move into Mesopotamia and take some cities.

Ziggurat of Ur-nammu

2141 B.C. Gudea takes the throne of Lagash. Ambitious temple-building program at Girsu.

2112 B.C. Ur-nammu of Ur tries to re-create the Agade Empire. He builds the famous ziggurat of Ur.

2500 B.C.   2200 B.C.   2100 B.C.

Centers of Civilization

BEFORE THE RISE of the great empires in Mesopotamia, there were many small city-states, each with its own ruler and god. Each state consisted of a city and the surrounding countryside and was the center of a brilliant civilization. Uruk, in the south, was the first to become important.

Around 2300 B.C., Sargon, a usurper, conquered all the cities of Mesopotamia and several beyond, creating the world's first empire. After his dynasty died out in about 2150 B.C., the kings of Ur, a city near the Gulf, tried to re-create Sargon's empire, but with limited success. About 100 years later, Ur fell to the Elamites, invaders from ancient Iran. A nomadic people called the Amorites gradually moved into Mesopotamia and took over the old Sumerian cities, including Babylon, and several of their chiefs became king. The sixth king of Babylon was Hammurabi, famous for his collection of laws.

In the 1500s B.C., the Kassites took over Babylonia and ruled well for 400 years. Meanwhile, in the north, the Assyrian Empire had grown from its beginnings in the city-state of Ashur in the third millennium B.C. It developed slowly over 2,000 years and reached a glorious peak around 645 B.C. The empire crumbled when the Babylonians conquered their key cities in 612 B.C. Babylonia became the most powerful empire in the known world until conquered by the Persian king, Cyrus, in 539 B.C.

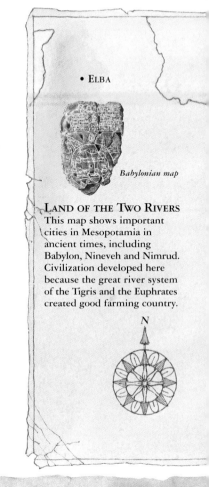

• ELBA

Babylonian map

LAND OF THE TWO RIVERS
This map shows important cities in Mesopotamia in ancient times, including Babylon, Nineveh and Nimrud. Civilization developed here because the great river system of the Tigris and the Euphrates created good farming country.

N

TIMELINE 2050–1000 B.C.

2004 B.C. Ibbi-Sin, last king of Ur, is captured by Elamites and taken to Susa.

2000 B.C. Fall of the Sumerian Empire. Amorites interrupt trade routes. Ur attacked by Elamites and falls. Assyria becomes independent and establishes trading network in Anatolia.

1900 B.C. Amorite chiefs take over some cities as rulers.

1792 B.C. Hammurabi, an Amorite ruler, becomes King of Babylon.

Hammurabi

1787 B.C. King Hammurabi conquers the major southern city of Isin.

1763 B.C. Hammurabi conquers the city of Larsa.

1761 B.C. Hammurabi conquers Mari and Eshnunna and may have conquered the city of Ashur.

1740 B.C. Expansion of the Hittite kingdom in Anatolia, based on the city of Hattusas.

Scorpion man

1595 B.C. The Hittite king, Mursulis, conquers North Syria. Marching further south, he destroys Babylon but does not take over the city.

1570 B.C. The Kassites, a foreign dynasty, begin a 400-year rule of peace and prosperity. King Kurigalzu builds a new capital city, naming it after himself. Babylon becomes a world power on an equal level with the kingdom of Egypt.

2050 B.C.   1790 B.C.   1600 B.C.   1500BC

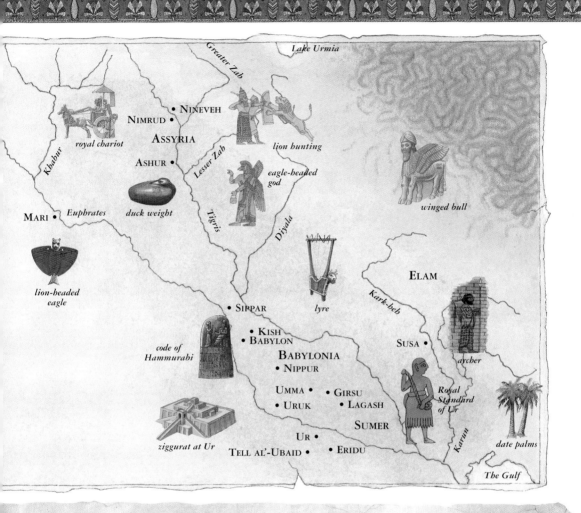

Lake Urmia

Greater Zab

NINEVEH

NIMRUD

ASSYRIA

royal chariot

lion hunting

ASHUR

Lesser Zab

eagle-headed
god

winged bull

Khabur

MARI   Euphrates   duck weight

Tigris

Diyala

lion-headed
eagle

lyre

ELAM

Kark-heh

SIPPAR

KISH
BABYLON

SUSA

code of
Hammurabi

BABYLONIA
NIPPUR

archer

UMMA   GIRSU
URUK   LAGASH

Royal
Standard
of Ur

SUMER

ziggurat at Ur

UR

TELL AL'-UBAID   ERIDU

Karun

date palms

The Gulf

1500 B.C. Mitanni, a new state, develops
to the north of Mesopotamia. The people
speak Hurrian and fight in
two-wheeled horse-drawn chariots.
They conquer land from the
Mediterranean to the Zagros Mountains,
including Assyria.

1365 B.C. Ashur-uballit becomes King
of Assyria and gains Assyria's
independence from Mitanni.

1150 B.C. The Elamites conquer Babylon,
ending Kassite rule.

copper peg

1124 B.C. Nebuchadnezzar I, a
later king of Babylon,
successfully attacks Elam,
bringing back
large amounts of booty,
including the statue of Marduk, the
Babylonian god the Elamites had
captured some years earlier.

1115 B.C. Tiglath-pileser I becomes
king. He expands Assyrian territory
and captures Babylon and other
southern cities. First written
account of the royal hunt in
Mesopotamia. Egyptian king

sends him a crocodile as a present.
1076 B.C. Death of Tiglath-pileser I.

1050 B.C. Ashurnasirpal I becomes king.

1000 B.C. Assyria is attacked by
many enemies, including the
nomadic Aramaeans, who
move into Mesopotamia and
take over large
areas. Their language,
Aramaic, and its alphabetic
script gradually replace
Akkadian and cuneiform.

Humbaba the giant

1130 B.C.   1100 B.C.   1000 B.C.

History Makers

T HE NAMES OF Mesopotamian kings are known because their victories and other achievements were recorded on clay tablets and palace wall decorations. The kings wanted to be sure that the gods knew that they had ruled well, and that their names would be remembered for ever. The names of ordinary soldiers and temple builders, the craftsmen who created the beautiful painted wall reliefs and the authors of the sagas and histories were not written down. Some astrologers, army commanders and state officials are known by name because they wrote letters to the king.

SARGON OF AGADE
(2334-2279 B.C.)
The man who created the world's first empire, by conquering all the cities of Sumer, Mari and Ebla. He founded the city of Agade, no trace of which has yet been found. A legend tells that when Sargon was a baby, his mother put him in a reed basket and set him afloat on a river. The man who found him trained him to be a gardener. When Sargon grew up, it was believed that he had been favored by the goddess Ishtar, and he became cup-bearer to the king of Kish (a city north of Babylon).

EANNATUM OF LAGASH
(C. 2440 B.C.)
A king of Lagash, a city in southern Sumer, who was a great warrior and temple-builder. His victory over the nearby state of Umma was recorded on the Vulture Stela, a limestone carving that showed vultures pecking at the bodies of dead soldiers.

ENHEDUANNA(C. 2250 B.C.)
The daughter of King Sargon of Agade is one of the few women in Mesopotamian history whose name is known. She held the important post of high priestess to the Moon-god at Ur. Her hymn to the god made her the first known woman author.

TIMELINE 950 B.C.-500 B.C.

911 B.C. Adad-nirari becomes king. Assyria recovers some of her lost possessions and defeats the Aramaeans and Babylon.

879 B.C. Ashurnasirpal II holds a banquet to celebrate the opening of his new palace at Nimrud.

858 B.C. Shalmaneser III, son of Ashurnasirpal II, spends most of his 34-year reign at war, campaigning in Syria, Phoenicia, Urartu and the Zagros Mountains.

Stela of Ashurnasirpal II

c. 845 B.C. Palace of Balawat built.

744 B.C. Tiglath-pileser III brings more territory under direct Assyrian control. Deportation of conquered peoples begins.

721 B.C. Sargon II decorates his palace at Khorsabad with carved reliefs showing his battle victories.

Black obelisk of Shalmaneser III

705 B.C. Sennacherib becomes king of Assyria.

701 B.C. Sennacherib attacks Hezekiah in Jerusalem.

694 B.C. Ashur-nadin-shumi rules Babylon on behalf of his father Sennacherib. He is captured by the Elamites and taken to Susa. In revenge, Sennacherib burns Babylon to the ground.

Balawat Gates

950 B.C.   850 B.C.   710 B.C.   690 B.C.

ASHURBANIPAL OF ASSYRIA (669-631 B.C.)

A great warrior king, who reigned at the peak of the Assyrian Empire. Ashurbanipal fought successfully against the Elamites, Babylonians and Arabs, and even made Egypt part of his empire for a time. But his greatest gift to civilization was the vast library in his palaces at Nineveh. Here, over 25,000 clay tablets were collected, including letters, legends and astronomical, mathematical and medical works.

NEBUCHADNEZZAR II (604-562 B.C.)

As crown prince, Nebuchadnezzar fought at the side of his father, the king of Babylon, and brought the Assyrian Empire to an end. Under his own rule, the Babylonians conquered neighboring countries, such as Palestine, and became one of the world powers of the time. Nebuchadnezzar built great fortifying walls around the city of Babylon and a magnificent ziggurat. He features in the Bible, as the king who captured Jerusalem and sent the people of Judah into captivity.

HAMMURABI (1792-1750 B.C.)

The king of Babylon who collected 282 laws concerning family, town and business life and had them recorded on a black stela, a large stone. Other rulers had made laws, but his is the largest collection to survive. The picture shows Shamash, god of justice, giving Hammurabi the symbols of kingship. Toward the end of his reign, he went to war and created an empire, but it did not last long after his death.

681 B.C. Sennacherib killed by his eldest son. His youngest son Esarhaddon becomes king.

671 B.C. Esarhaddon invades Egypt and captures the Egyptian capital of Memphis.

668 B.C. Ashurbanipal becomes king of Assyria. His brother Shamash-shum-ukin becomes king of Babylon.

Tiglath-pileser III

664 B.C. Ashurbanipal invades Egypt and destroys the southern city of Thebes.

663 or 653 B.C. Ashurbanipal begins a series of wars with Elam.

652 B.C. Rebellion of Shamash-shum-ukin. Ashurbanipal invades Babylonia.

648 B.C. Ashurbanipal lays siege to Babylon, which suffers starvation.

631 B.C. Death of Ashurbanipal. Assyrian Empire begins to collapse.

Nimrud

612 B.C. Babylonians attack and burn the Assyrian cities of Nimrud and Nineveh.

605 B.C. Assyrians defeated by the Babylonians at the battle of Carchemish.

Ashurbanipal on horseback

604 B.C. Nebuchadnezzar II becomes King of Babylon, and Babylon becomes a world power.

562 B.C. Nebuchadnezzar II dies.

539 B.C. Cyrus of Persia takes Babylon.

663 B.C.   620 B.C.   500 B.C.

A Legendary King

GIANT ATTACK
The giant Humbaba guarded the Cedar Forest, far away, in Lebanon. His voice was like thunder, his breath was fire, and he could hear the faintest noise from far away. To test their courage, Gilgamesh and Enkidu decided to kill this monster. They were terrified by the giant's dreadful face and taunting words, but finally cut off his head with one stroke.

THE ADVENTURES of one king of ancient Sumer were so exciting that they became the subject of some of the oldest stories in the world. Gilgamesh was king of Uruk, one of the most important cities of ancient Sumer, probably around 2700 B.C. He was said to be two-thirds god and one-third human and seems to have become a legend in his own lifetime.

His deeds were first written down about 4,000 years ago and recounted in stories and poems over many generations, passing from the Sumerians to the Babylonians and Assyrians. Finally, in the 7th century B.C., the Assyrians wove the individual tales together into an exciting adventure story called an epic and wrote it down on clay tablets. The *Epic of Gilgamesh* was stored in the great libraries of King Ashurbanipal of Assyria, where it was discovered by archaeologists over 100 years ago.

Gilgamesh was not a good king at first, so the gods created Enkidu, a wild, hairy man, to fight him. The king realized he had met his match, and the two then became good friends and went everywhere together.

THE BULL OF HEAVEN
Ishtar, the goddess of love and war (on the left), tries to stop Enkidu and Gilgamesh from killing the Bull of Heaven. Ishtar had fallen in love with the hero-king, and she wanted to marry him. Gilgamesh knew that the goddess was fickle, and turned her down. Ishtar was furious and asked her father, Anu the sky god, to give her the Bull of Heaven so she could take revenge on Gilgamesh. The Bull was a deadly beast who had the power to bring death and long-term misery to the city of Uruk. The two friends fought and killed the bull. Enkidu (on the right) hung on to its tail, as Gilgamesh delivered the death blow with his sword.

THE CITY OF URUK

There is very little of Uruk left today, but it was a very important city when Gilgamesh was king. The city had splendid temples dedicated to Anu, the sky god, and his daughter Ishtar who fell in love with Gilgamesh. The king also built a great wall around the city. When his friend Enkidu died, Gilgamesh was heartbroken, and also frightened because he realized he would die one day, too. He wanted to live forever. In the end, he decided that creating a beautiful city was his best chance of immortality. He would be remembered forever for creating the fine temples and massive walls of Uruk.

THE PLANT OF ETERNAL LIFE

A massive stone carving of a heroic figure found in the palace of King Sargon II may be of Gilgamesh. The hero set out to find Utnapishtim, the ruler of another Sumerian city who was said to have found the secret of eternal life. The way was long and dangerous, and led into the mountains where lions prowled. The moon god protected Gilgamesh and led him to a great mountain, with a gate guarded by scorpion men. After a terrifying walk in total darkness, Gilgamesh emerged on the other side of the mountain into the garden of the gods. Beyond the garden were the Waters of Death, but our hero found a ferryman to take him safely across. At last he met Utnapishtim, who told him he would never die if he found a plant that grew on the sea bed. Gilgamesh tied stones on his feet, dived into the sea and picked the plant. However, on the way home, he stooped down to drink at a pool. A water snake appeared and snatched the plant. With it went Gilgamesh's hope of immortality.

LASTING FAME

The figures on this stone vase from Uruk probably show Gilgamesh. The king found the lasting fame he wanted because his name lived on in stories and legends, as well as in statues and carvings such as this.

CLAY TABLET

Writing was done on clay tablets with a stylus (pen) made from a reed. The writer pressed the stylus into a slab of damp clay. This was left to dry and harden. The clay tablet in the picture, from around 3000 B.C., has symbols on it. One symbol looks like a hand, and others resemble trees or plants. It is not clear which language they represent, although it is likely to be Sumerian.

The Development of Writing

MESOPOTAMIA WAS ONE OF the first places in the world to develop writing. The earliest examples are about 5,000 years old and come from the Sumerian city-state of Uruk. At first, writing was in the form of pictures and numbers, as a useful way to make lists of produce such as barley, wine and cheese, or numbers of cattle and donkeys. Gradually, this picture-writing was replaced by groups of wedge-shaped strokes, arranged in different ways. This type of writing is called cuneiform, which means 'wedge-shaped,' because of the shape the reed pen made as it was pressed into the clay. To begin with, cuneiform writing was only used to write Sumerian, but later it was adapted to write several other languages, including Assyrian and Babylonian.

TWO SCRIBES

The scribe on the right is writing on a clay tablet with a stylus. He is making a list of all the booty and prisoners that his king has captured in battle. He is writing in Akkadian, one of the languages used by the Assyrians. The other scribe is writing on a leather roll, possibly in Aramaic, another language the Assyrians used. Aramaic was an easier language to write because it used an alphabet, unlike Akkadian, which used about 600 different signs.

SHAPES AND SIZES

Differently shaped clay tablets, including prisms and cylinders, were used for writing. Many tablets were flat but some were three-dimensional and hollow like vases. One like this, that narrows at each end, is called a prism. It is about 12 inches long and records the military campaigns of King Sargon of Assyria.

A CLAY TABLET

You will need: pen, thick cardboard, ruler, scissors, modeling clay, cutting board, rolling pin, blunt knife, paper, paint and paintbrush, cloth.

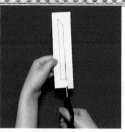

1 Draw a pointed stylus 7¾ in. x ½ in. on to the cardboard with the pen. Use the shape in the picture as a guide. Cut the shape out with the scissors.

2 Roll out the clay on the cutting board with the rolling pin until it measures about 12 in. x 6 in. Use the knife to cut out the clay as shown.

3 Take your card stylus and start writing cuneiform script on your clay tablet. Use the wedge shape of your stylus to make the strokes.

WRITING DEVELOPMENT

Cuneiform signs gradually came to be used for ideas as well as objects. At first, a drawing of a head meant simply 'head,' but later it came to mean 'front' and 'first.' The symbols also came to represent spoken sounds and could be used to make new words. For example, in English, you could make the word 'belief' by drawing the symbols for a bee and a leaf. The chart shows how cuneiform writing developed. On the top row are simple drawings. In the middle row the pictures have been replaced by groups of wedges, and in the bottom row are the even more simplified versions of the signs.

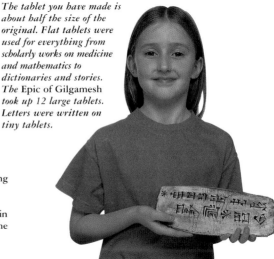

The tablet you have made is about half the size of the original. Flat tablets were used for everything from scholarly works on medicine and mathematics to dictionaries and stories. The Epic of Gilgamesh *took up 12 large tablets. Letters were written on tiny tablets.*

WRITING ON THE ROCK FACE

Henry Rawlinson, a British army officer who helped decipher cuneiform in the mid-1800s, risks his life climbing a cliff face at Behistun to copy the writing there. The inscription was in three languages, Old Persian, Elamite and Babylonian (Akkadian). He guessed that the cuneiform signs in Old Persian represented letters of the alphabet and found the name of Darius, the King of Persia. This helped scholars work out all three languages.

4 Copy the wedge shapes of the cuneiform script shown here. See how each group of strokes combines to make a particular letter or word.

5 Move your tablet on to a piece of clean paper. Take the paintbrush and paint and cover the clay, working the paint well into the cuneiform script.

6 When the painting is finished, wipe across the clay with the cloth. Most of the paint should come off, leaving the lettering a darker color.

7 Let the clay and the paint dry. The lettering on your finished tablet reads: Nebuchadnezzar King of Babylon

Seals and Impressions

A SEAL IS A small piece of a hard material, usually stone, with a raised or sunken design on it. When this design is rolled across soft clay, it leaves an impression in the clay. In Mesopotamia, seals were impressed on to lumps of clay that sealed jars of wine or oil. Sometimes the clay was attached to ropes which tied up boxes or baskets. Seals were also rolled across clay writing tablets and their clay envelopes. Impressions in the clay identified who owned the object and made it harder to pass on stolen goods. Seals were often worn as jewelry, as part of a necklace or worn like a brooch. People thought seals also had magical powers that would protect them from illness and other dangers. They sometimes included pictures of the gods for added protection.

PERSONAL STAMP
This is the base of a long cylinder-shaped seal. It also has a design which the owner could use to stamp his or her mark on to objects. The base of a cylinder might only be ¼ inch in diameter, which made cylinders very hard to carve. Perhaps this seal once belonged to a priest since it shows a priest performing a ritual.

ROLLING DESIGN
Most seals were cylindrical in shape so that designs could be rolled over a clay tablet and repeated several times. This design shows the storm god, Adad, brandishing his special symbol, forked lightning. The seal was made in Babylon around 600 B.C. It is made of lapis lazuli, and is 4¾ inches long about four times as long as most cylinder seals.

MIRROR IMAGE
A design showing a king or official being led by a goddess into the presence of a great god was a common design on cylinder seals. The design was cut into the seal the opposite way around to the way it would look when it was rolled out.

A CYLINDER SEAL
You will need: cutting board, rolling pin, self-hardening clay, ruler, paintbrush, glue, cardboard roll, scissors, toothpick, clay or plasticine.

1 Take the cutting board, rolling pin and self-hardening clay. Carefully roll out the clay until it measures roughly 6 in. x 6 in. Trim one edge.

2 Apply glue onto the outside of the cardboard roll. Place the glued roll onto the clay and carefully cover the roll with the clay.

3 Make sure the roll is completely covered with clay. Trim away the excess clay at the edges. Smooth over the joint of the clay with your fingers.

ROLL IT OUT

Seals were rolled over clay, so that the design was repeated. Cylinder seals are known from about 3000 B.C. at Uruk, and at Susa in ancient Iran. Various kinds of stone, or glass, bone, shell, ivory or metal were shaped into cylinders. The length of the cylinder was then carved with intricate designs, either hand cut with flint or copper tools, or drilled with bow drills.

SHEEP SEAL

One of the earliest seals ever made comes from the city of Uruk. Its cylindrical base is carved out of a piece of limestone. The sheep-shaped knob on the top is made of copper. Nobody knows who invented the first cylinder seals but some people think they may have been made from the knuckle bones of sheep. Later designs copied the knuckle shape, complete with knobs.

The cylinder seal you have made is very much larger than those used in Mesopotamia. Cylinder seals were usually only ¼ or 1¼ inches tall and ¼ to ½ inches in diameter.

4 Use the toothpick to mark out a pattern in the clay. When you are happy with your pattern, you will use these marks as guides.

5 Following the marks made with the toothpick, use the end of a thin paintbrush to engrave your pattern deeply in the clay. Let harden.

6 Take the cutting board and rolling pin again. Roll out the second piece of clay, or plasticine, until it measures roughly 7¾ in. x 5½ in.

7 Make sure the clay on your cylinder seal is hard. Roll the seal across the clay or plasticine, pressing down firmly. Watch the pattern appear!

Gods and Goddesses

THE PEOPLE OF MESOPOTAMIA had many gods and goddesses. Every city had a temple to its own chief deity (god), and there were often temples dedicated to other members of the god's family too. The Sumerians and Akkadian-speaking peoples who lived in Mesopotamia worshiped the same gods and goddesses, but had different names for them. The Assyrians and Babylonians also worshiped these gods. The Sumerians called the moon god Nanna, but in Akkadian his name was Sin. The chief Sumerian god was called Enlil, who was often also referred to as King, Supreme Lord, Father, or Creator. According to one Sumerian poem, no one was allowed to look at Enlil, not even the other gods. The Mesopotamian kings believed they had been chosen by Enlil.

The god's chief sanctuary was at the city of Nippur. Legends tell that when the Nippur temple was raided by the army of the King of Agade, Enlil was so angry that he caused the Agade dynasty to come to an end. Enlil owned the Tablets of Destiny, which were thought to control the fates of people and the other gods.

GODDESS
This statue of a goddess was found in pieces at the palace of Mari on the River Euphrates. Two goddesses like her, pouring water from vases, were part of a scene on the walls of the palace courtyard. The painting showed a king being invested with royal power by Ishtar, the goddess of love and war.

BEFORE THE GOD
A scene on a 4,000-year-old seal shows an official called Lamabazi being led into the presence of a great god by a lesser god. The great god is sitting on the throne, and before him is a brazier for burning incense. Lamabazi is holding his hand in front of his face as a sign of respect for the god.

IN THE BEGINNING
Marduk was the god of Babylon. He is shown here standing on his mushushshu (snake dragon). In the *Epic of Creation*, a Babylonian story about how Marduk created the world, he fought against a female monster, Tiamat, and her son, Kingu. After Marduk had killed them, the other gods made him their king. Marduk then brought the rest of creation into existence. He made models of human beings by mixing some clay with the blood of Kingu and then brought them to life.

CLUES TO IDENTITY

Most of our ideas about what the Mesopotamian gods and goddesses looked like come from their pictures on cylinder seals. This one shows Ishtar, the goddess of love and war, carrying her weapons. She is accompanied by a lion, which was her sacred animal. Shamash, the sun god, is recognizable by the flames coming from him, as he rises between two mountains. Ea, the water god, has streams of water gushing from his shoulders.

GOD OF ASSYRIA

Ashur was the chief god of the Assyrians. It was thought that he was the god who chose the Assyrian kings and went before them into battle. He is often symbolized by the same horned cap as Enlil, the chief Sumerian god. Sometimes he is shown standing on a winged bull or on a mushushshu (snake dragon) like Marduk, the god of Babylon. Both gods were honored in New Year festivals when their priests slapped the reigning king's face, pulled his ears and made him bow low. The king then said he had served his people properly and was re-crowned for another year.

FERTILE MIND

Nisaba was originally a goddess of fertility and agriculture, although she later became the goddess of writing. Good harvests were very important to the people of Mesopotamia, and almost everyone ate barley bread and dates. This carving of Nisaba shows her covered with plants. She is wearing an elaborate headdress composed of a horned crown and ears of barley. Flowers sprout from her shoulders, and she is holding a bunch of dates.

Houses for the Gods

THERE WAS A TEMPLE at the center of every Mesopotamian city, which was regarded as the house of the local god or goddess. A statue of the deity was put in a special room in the temple, and daily ceremonies were held in his or her honor. One of the main duties of kings was to build or repair temples. King Gudea of Lagash built 15 temples in his city-state. One was inspired by a dream in which the king saw a huge man with two lions and a woman with a writing tablet. Another man appeared with a temple plan, a basket and a brick mold. A dream interpreter told Gudea that the man was the god Ningirsu and the woman was Nisaba, the goddess of writing. This dream meant that Ningirsu wanted Gudea to build him a temple.

TEMPLE BUILDER
King Gudea was one of the great Mesopotamian temple builders. He described the process of building the temple to Ningirsu, near Lagash, on two large clay cylinders. Before installing the god's statue, he purified the temple by surrounding it with fire and anointing the temple platform with aromatic balm. Next day the king washed himself and offered prayers and sacrifices. Finally, the statue was taken to its temple with great ceremony.

FORMER GLORY
All that is left today of the ziggurat (temple-tower) at Ur is the lowest level. In 2100 B.C. it was a three-staged tower built of mud-brick. Three staircases met at the top of the first stage, and the worshippers went on up a single staircase to the temple at the top. Ziggurats may have developed their stepped structure because new temples were often built on top of old ones, and so a huge platform gradually built up. Ziggurats were first built by King Ur-nammu of Ur.

MAKE A ZIGGURAT

You will need: thick cardboard, ruler, pencil, scissors, masking tape, glue, paints and large and small paintbrushes.

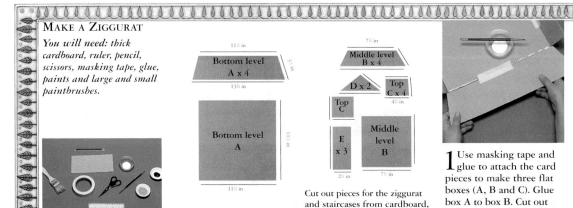

Bottom level A x 4 — 11¾ in — 13¾ in — 3½ in

Bottom level A — 11¼ in — 11 in

Middle level B x 4 — 7½ in

D x 2 — Top C x 4 — 4½ in

Top C

E x 3 — 2½ in

Middle level B — 7½ in

Cut out pieces for the ziggurat and staircases from cardboard, as shown above.

1 Use masking tape and glue to attach the card pieces to make three flat boxes (A, B and C). Glue box A to box B. Cut out three doorways in box C.

FOOD FIT FOR THE GODS

The building on this clay impression may be the ziggurat at Babylon, where the seal was found. The figure of a man seems to be offering a sacrifice. The people of Mesopotamia believed they had been created to serve the gods so they gave them special food, including fish, meat, cream, honey, cakes and beer.

THE TOWER OF BABEL

The ziggurat of Marduk, the protector god of Babylon, was thought by modern Westerners to be the Tower of Babel mentioned in the Bible. This is an imaginary picture of the tower the Babylonians built to get closer to heaven. The story says God was angry with them for thinking the way to heaven was so simple. He made the builders speak different languages so they could not understand each other and finish the work.

LAYING THE FOUNDATIONS

A statuette and clay tablet of Ur-nammu of Ur show that the king took his temple-building duties seriously. To make sure the gods knew who had built temples for them, the kings put a clay or stone tablet beneath each of the four corners of the temple, with their names on. They often also put statues of themselves like this one, complete with bricks and carrying a brick basket. Ur-nammu built temples at Ur and several other cities.

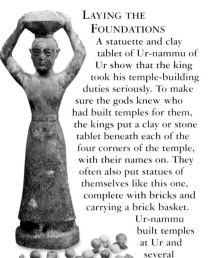

A real ziggurat was a solid stepped temple-tower of mud-brick. Worshipers climbed the stairways to the god's shrine on the top. It is sometimes seen as a ladder between heaven and earth.

2 Cut out four pieces of card 3½ in. x ¼ in., and cut out the edge as shown in the picture. Glue them on top of box C. Then glue box C on top of the ziggurat.

3 Glue triangles D to the first strip E for the main staircase. Cut out two triangles of cardboard for the side stairs and glue them to the other two strips E.

4 Glue the staircases into position as shown. Add strips of cardboard for more doorways and the sides of the main staircase. When dry, paint the ziggurat brown.

5 When completely dry, add details such as the stairs on the staircases and the markings on the sandstone, with black paint and a fine brush.

Sumerian Burial

W HEN the Sumerian city of Ur was excavated in the 1930s, archaeologists found hundreds of graves. The discovery gave an insight into how the inhabitants regarded death and burial. Little evidence about death rituals in other parts of Mesopotamia survives.

In Ur, most people seem to have been buried in family graves under the courtyards of their houses. Their children were put in jars and placed in chapels above the family graves. Other people were buried in the city cemetery. Most bodies had been wrapped in reed mats or placed in baskets (which no longer existed but the patterns of their weaving were pressed into the soil). Most people had a few belongings buried with them, but 17 of the graves contained many precious objects. They may have belonged to kings and queens, and so were called the Royal Graves.

FIT FOR THE QUEEN'S COURT
A headdress of gold and semiprecious stones, with finely worked golden leaves and ribbons, was found in the grave of Queen Pu-abi at Ur. It may have belonged to one of the ladies of her court. The body of the queen herself was bedecked in gold earrings, finger rings and necklaces. Tiny threads of wool suggested that she had been wrapped in a red woolen cloak.

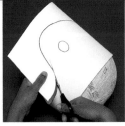

CEREMONIAL HELMET

An exquisitely decorated helmet of electrum (a mixture of gold and silver) may have belonged to Meskalamdug, whose name was found on two golden bowls in the grave. The wig-like pattern is hammered from the inside. The holes around the edge were provided so that a lining could be sewn in to make it more comfortable.

RAM IN THE THICKET
No one knows why this ram was placed in a mass grave called the Great Death Pit. A pair of rams or goats in a thicket was a common image in Mesopotamian art. This ram was one of a pair. It was made of wood decorated with bright blue lapis lazuli to show the animal's hairy coat and a silver plate over its belly.

A GOLD HELMET

You will need: balloon, flour, water and newspaper strips to make papier mâché, scissors, thick card stock 23½ in. x 7¼ in., masking tape, pen, pieces of white cotton fabric, glue, string, gold and black paint and paintbrushes.

1 Blow up the balloon until it is as big as your head. Dip newspaper strips in flour-and-water paste, and cover the balloon with layers of papier mâché.

2 When the papier mâché is completely dry, pop the balloon. Trim the edge of the helmet. Attach the piece of card stock to the helmet with masking tape.

3 With the pen, draw the shape of the sides of the helmet as shown. Cut around the shape with the scissors. Draw and cut out holes for the ears.

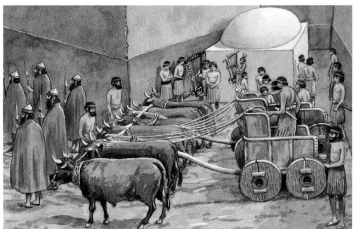

ROYAL FUNERAL

The bodies of six guards and 68 court ladies were found in a grave at Ur called the Great Death Pit. Woolley thought they were the servants of kings and queens who had been chosen to accompany them to the afterlife. They walked down into the grave in a great funeral procession. Then they drank a poisoned drink and fell asleep never to wake again.

You have made a copy of Meskalamdug's ceremonial helmet. One meant for real use would have been made of a stronger metal such as copper.

GOLDEN TABLEWARE

So many beautiful golden objects, such as these fluted bowls and glasses, were found in certain graves at Ur that Woolley called them the Royal Graves. In 1989, the tombs of some Assyrian queens were found under the palace floor at Nimrud. The queens were buried with their exquisite jewelry of gold, but unlike Queen Pu-abi of Ur they were not buried with their servants.

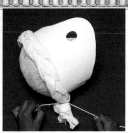

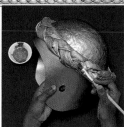

4 Take three strips of white fabric 39¼ in. x 1½ in. Tie them together with a knot at one end and braid the three strips loosely and knot the other end.

5 Glue the braid around the helmet, covering the joint between the papier mâché and card stock as shown. Tie off the end with string to make a tail.

6 Paint the whole helmet, inside and out, with gold paint. Use a broad paintbrush. Paint over the cloth braid, too. Allow the paint to dry thoroughly.

7 Add detail of hair to the helmet using the black paint and a fine paintbrush. You can use Meskalamdug's helmet to give you some ideas!

21

Education

Sᴄʜᴏᴏʟ ʙᴜɪʟᴅɪɴɢs in Mesopotamia looked very similar to ordinary houses. Archaeologists have been able to identify the schools because large numbers of clay tablets containing mistakes and corrections were found there. The tablets had been corrected by the teachers just as modern teachers mark books. A school was called an edubba, which means tablet house.

The tablets show which subjects were taught and how schools were run. The head teacher was called ummia (expert), but was also known as the school father. The teachers' job was to write out tablets for students to copy, to correct their exercises and listen to them recite what they had learned by heart.

The school day was very long, lasting from sunrise to sunset. Discipline was very strict. One boy was caned several times in one day—for getting his clothes dirty, making a mistake on his tablet and talking in class.

Mᴜsɪᴄ Lᴇssᴏɴs
Students learned music at school. In examinations they were asked questions about playing musical instruments, different types of songs and how to conduct a choir. This figure showing a man playing a lyre is on a highly decorated box called the Royal Standard of Ur because it was once thought it was a standard that was carried into battle.

Lᴇᴀʀɴɪɴɢ ᴀʙᴏᴜᴛ Hᴇʀᴏᴇs
When students were good at reading and writing, they studied the Mesopotamian myths and legends, such as the stories of the heroic king of Uruk, Gilgamesh, and his friend Enkidu.

Cɪᴠɪʟ Sᴇʀᴠᴀɴᴛ
Ebih-il was Superintendent of the Palace at Mari. The main aim of schools was to produce scribes and civil servants like Ebih-il. Some students became scholars who worked in the temple and royal libraries, or teachers. At school, boys learned the two main languages, Sumerian and Akkadian, by copying and learning by heart groups of related words. They also studied other subjects, such as botany and zoology, by copying lists of plants, animals, insects and birds.

Exᴄʟᴜsɪᴠᴇ Eᴅᴜᴄᴀᴛɪᴏɴ
If these modern-day Iraqi boys had been born 5,000 years ago, they would probably not have gone to school. Only boys from prominent families went to school in ancient Mesopotamia. They were the sons of important officials, officers in the army, sea captains or scribes.

PLAYING WITH NUMBERS

Math was very important in Mesopotamian schools. Clay tablets, such as this one, had mathematical problems written on them. Some of these related to practical matters, but most were just brainteasers. The Mesopotamians obviously liked playing with numbers. Students also had tables for multiplying and dividing, and for working out squares and square roots. There were two number systems, one using 10 as a base and the other, 60. We use 10 as a base too, and 60 to measure time, for example.

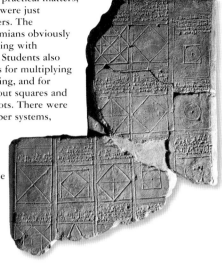

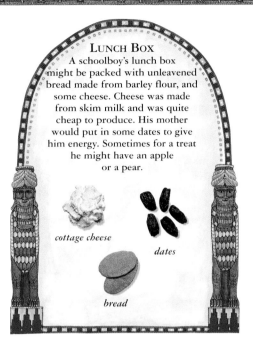

LUNCH BOX

A schoolboy's lunch box might be packed with unleavened bread made from barley flour, and some cheese. Cheese was made from skim milk and was quite cheap to produce. His mother would put in some dates to give him energy. Sometimes for a treat he might have an apple or a pear.

cottage cheese

dates

bread

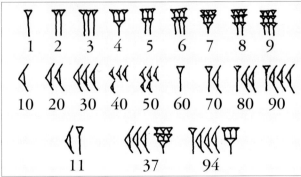

1	2	3	4	5	6	7	8	9
10	20	30	40	50	60	70	80	90

11	37	94

WRITING NUMBERS

This chart shows how numbers were written in Mesopotamia. Numbers were written on clay tablets using a system of wedge-shaped signs. For the numbers 1 to 9 the appropriate number of wedges was arranged in groups. Ten was one slanting wedge, 20 two slanting wedges, and so on up to 50. The figure 60 was written with an upright wedge. There was no sign for zero. The same symbol is used for the numbers 1 and 60. You can tell which number is which by looking at the order of the wedges. For example, if the slanting wedge comes first the number is 11 (10+1). If the slanting wedge comes afterward the number is 70 (60+10).

PRINCE'S EDUCATION

Learning to drive a chariot and fight in battle were part of King Ashurbanipal's education when he was crown prince. Officials taught him the Sumerian and Akkadian languages, which he found difficult. He also studied multiplication and division, astronomy and ancient literature, and learned to ride a horse and hunt.

Music and Games

SEVEN-STRINGED HARP
Harps and lyres were two of the most popular musical instruments in Mesopotamia. They were sometimes played in funeral processions. The harp on this Babylonian terracotta relief has seven strings, which were probably made from animal gut.

INSTRUMENTAL MUSIC and singing played an important part in Mesopotamian life. Musicians entertained at the court of the king and played in temple rituals. King Gudea of Lagash wrote a learned work about music. Most of the musical works that have come down to us are hymns to gods and kings. For example, we know that Sargon of Agade's daughter, Enheduanna, composed a hymn to the moon god at Ur. People may have amused themselves with music, singing and dancing in their homes and in the market place. One Sumerian poem about the goddess Inanna and her lover Dumuzi speaks about them going to see an entertainer singing and dancing in the public square. In the Middle East today, musicians and storytellers still entertain in the open squares of cities.

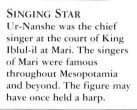

ROYAL GAME OF UR
A beautiful board game was found in the Royal Graves of Ur. It is made from wood covered in bitumen (tar) and decorated with a mosaic of shell, bone, blue lapis lazuli, red glass and pink limestone. The game may have been a bit like Ludo, with two sets of counters and four-sided dice, but the rules have not been found!

SINGING STAR
Ur-Nanshe was the chief singer at the court of King Iblul-il at Mari. The singers of Mari were famous throughout Mesopotamia and beyond. The figure may have once held a harp.

MAKE A LYRE

You will need: pencil, thin cardboard, scissors, 3 pieces of dowel 21½ in. long, masking tape, glue, flour, water and newspaper strips for papier mâché, sandpaper, paints and paintbrushes, pins, piece of balsa wood, string or rubber bands.

1 Draw a bull shape 15¾ in. long x 10 in. wide onto the cardboard, following the shape shown above. You will need two of these cardboard cutouts. Cut out two horns.

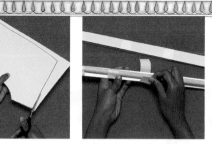

2 Cut four cardboard strips 1 in. x 21½ in. Use masking tape and glue to attach a strip to each side of two of the pieces of dowel.

3 Attach the two dowel pieces to one of the bull shapes, one coming out of the head, the other out of the rump. Tape the other bull shape on top.

DRUMS AND CYMBALS

Musicians pictured on a palace wall are playing cymbals and a drum as well as stringed instruments. There were several kinds of drums in Babylonia. One was the balag, which was shaped like an hour-glass. It was used in temple rituals to soothe the gods. Another was the lilissu, which was set up in temple courtyards and beaten when there was an eclipse of the Moon. Flutes were also played. Just over a hundred years ago a Babylonian clay whistle was found. Unfortunately it has now been lost.

CEREMONY WITH MUSIC

Musicians play in victory celebrations. They are playing at a ceremony to celebrate King Ashurbanipal's victory over the King of Elam. Musicians took part in other rituals too, such as one after a lion hunt when Assyrian kings offered the dead animals to the gods.

Your lyre is like one found in the Royal Graves of Ur. It was made of wood and decorated with a mosaic in shells, blue lapis lazuli and limestone. The bull's head was made of gold and lapis lazuli with ivory horns. It had 11 strings.

4 Use masking tape to attach the horns. Make a flour-and-water paste and use papier mâché to fill the gap between the two bull shapes and cover the bull.

5 Take the third piece of dowel and tape it to the top of the other two pieces. Smooth with sandpaper and paint. Add cardboard pegs as shown and paint.

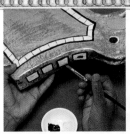

6 When the papier mâché is dry, decorate the body of the lyre with the paints. Use different colored paints to create an inlaid mosaic effect.

7 Cut 7 strings from string or rubber bands. Tie them to the balsa wood and pin it on the bull's body. Tie the other end of the strings to the top piece of dowel.

Family Life

LIFE WAS HARD for ordinary families in Mesopotamia. Many babies and young children died from disease or because of poor maternity care. Boys from poorer families did not go to school but worked with their fathers, who taught them their trades. Girls stayed at home with their mothers and learned how to keep house and look after the younger children. Some of the details of family life are described in ancient clay tablets. In one tablet, a boy rudely tells his mother to hurry up and make his lunch. In another one, a boy is scared of what his father will say when he sees his bad school report.

In some ways, Mesopotamian society was quite modern. The law said that women could own property and get a divorce. However, if a woman was unable to have a baby, she had to agree to her husband taking a second wife. The second wife and her children had rights too. They remained part of the household even if the first wife had a child after all.

MOTHERHOOD
Having lots of healthy children, especially sons, was very important because families needed children to grow up and work for them. Most women stayed at home to look after their families. Women did not usually go out to work, but some had jobs as priestesses. Some priestesses were single but others were married women.

HOUSEHOLD GOODS
Pottery was used in Mesopotamian homes from the time of the first villages. At first it was handmade, but later a potter's wheel was used. This pottery jug may have been modeled on a pitcher made of metal. Tools and utensils were made of stone or metal. There was not much furniture in a Mesopotamian house, just mud-brick benches for sitting or sleeping on. There may have been rugs and cushions to make the homes more homely and comfortable, but none has survived.

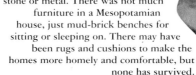

MODEL HOUSE
From models such as this one, we know that homes in Mesopotamia were similar to village houses in modern Iraq. They were built of mud-brick and were usually rectangular, with rooms around a central courtyard. Doors and windows were small to keep the house warm in the cold winters, and cool during the hot summers. Flat roofs, reached by stairs from the central court, could be used as an extra room in summer.

MESOPOTAMIAN FASHIONS

A statue of a worshiper found in a temple shows the dress of a Sumerian woman. Dresses were of sheepskin, sometimes with a sheepskin shawl as well, or of woolen cloth. One shoulder was left bare. Some women, who may have been priestesses, wore tall, elaborate hats like this one. Later fashions included long, fringed garments. Sumerian men wore sheepskin kilts, but men in the Assyrian and Babylonian Empires wore long, woolen tunics. Both sexes wore jewelry.

EARNING A LIVING

Most families in ancient Mesopotamia depended on agriculture for a living, just as many people in the Middle East do today. Farmers rented their land from bigger landowners, such as important officials, kings or temples, and had to pay part of what they produced in taxes. Many townspeople had jobs in local government or worked in the textile and metalwork industries.

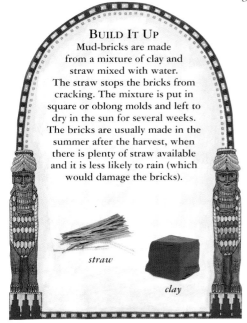

BUILD IT UP

Mud-bricks are made from a mixture of clay and straw mixed with water. The straw stops the bricks from cracking. The mixture is put in square or oblong molds and left to dry in the sun for several weeks. The bricks are usually made in the summer after the harvest, when there is plenty of straw available and it is less likely to rain (which would damage the bricks).

straw

clay

GONE FISHING

There were lots of fish in the rivers and ponds of ancient Iraq, and fish seem to have been an important part of people's diet. Fish bones were found at Eridu, in the south of Sumer, in the oldest level of the temple. Perhaps fish were offered to the water god Enki as an offering. (He is the god with streams of water containing fish springing out of his shoulders.) Some of the carved reliefs from the Assyrian palaces give us rare glimpses into everyday life and include little scenes of men going fishing.

A Woman's Life

MOST MESOPOTAMIAN WOMEN married in their early teens. Sometimes, two families agreed on a marriage when the future man and wife were still children. After the agreement was made, the children lived with their parents until they were old enough to set up home together. Then the young man took a betrothal present to his bride's family, such as some clothing, some silver and a ring. When the marriage took place, the wife's father would give her a dowry of jewelry, clothes or furniture to take to her new home. She might be given a field or an orchard as her property.

Some women had a lot of responsibility. Queen Shibtu, wife of King Zimri-lim of Mari, ran the palace while her husband was away and kept him informed about everything that went on.

A queen seems to have become important only after producing a son. The mother of a king often had higher status than his wife.

WOMEN'S RIGHTS
The laws of King Hammurabi of Babylon are carved on this stone pillar. They tell us about some of the legal rights held by women in Mesopotamia. They could own property and engage in business. A woman could get a divorce if her husband treated her badly. If she could prove her innocence, she could reclaim her dowry and return to her parents' home. But if she neglected her duties as a wife, the laws said she could be thrown into water.

OF ROYAL BLOOD
The fine clothes and jewelry on this statue show that it is a figure of a princess. She belonged to the family of King Gudea of Lagash. Her name was once written on her statue, but unfortunately it can no longer be read. The statue was found at Girsu, where King Gudea built his temples, so she may also have been a priestess.

MAKE A NECKLACE
You will need: self-hardening clay, toothpick, paper, pen, scissors, paintbrushes, glue, paints in bright colors, wire and pliers, strong thread.

1 Make a variety of beads using the self-hardening clay, in long shapes and round shapes. Use the toothpick to make a hole through each bead.

2 Cut shapes out of the paper following the pattern shown above. The shapes should be about 1 in. long. They will be used to make cylindrical beads.

3 Roll the pieces of paper tightly around a fine paintbrush as shown. Glue the tail of the paper to secure it to itself and let dry.

WOMEN'S WORK

A relief shows a woman spinning. A great deal is known about the women who worked at Mari, a city on the River Euphrates, because they are mentioned in letters that archaeologists found in the palace ruins. Many women worked in the textile industry. There were several female musicians. Other women worked in the royal kitchens, or were midwives who helped mothers in childbirth. The biggest surprise of all was to find that one woman was a doctor.

EDUCATING DUDU

Although usually only boys went to school, a few women were educated and became scribes, such as this woman, Dudu. There were nine women scribes at Mari. Their names appear on ration lists, showing that they were palace employees. We do not know how they trained.

EXPENSIVE NECKLACE

Only a rich woman would have worn a necklace like this, as it would have been quite expensive. The blue lapis lazuli was imported. It was mined in the mountains of Afghanistan and made into beads in workshops in Iran. The necklace was made about 4,500 years ago.

Your necklace would probably have been made of gold, blue lapis lazuli, red carnelian and limestone. People who could not afford these used a glassy material called paste to make beads.

4 When the beads are dry, paint them. If you are using different colors, allow the paint to dry thoroughly before adding the next coat.

5 Cut two small pieces of wire. Use the pliers to make two hooks. One side of each hook should be closed as shown, the other should be left open.

6 Tie a long piece of strong thread firmly to the closed side of one hook. Push the end of the thread through the painted beads to string the beads.

7 When you get to the end of the thread, or have used up all your beads, attach the end of the thread to the closed end of the second hook.

Farming

NORTHERN MESOPOTAMIA had enough rainfall to let farmers grow crops, but in the dry south, farmers had to use the Tigris and the Euphrates rivers to irrigate the land. The main crop was barley. Wooden plows were used to break up the soil before the seed was sown with seed drills. A Sumerian almanac or diary told farmers what they should do at various times of the year. Vegetables and fruit were also grown, dates being particularly valued. They also kept cattle, sheep and goats on the grasslands between the cultivated areas. The landscape looked much the same as it does today, although rivers have changed course over the years. The weather has always been unpredictable and sometimes crops are spoiled by sudden storms.

SHEPHERD WITH LAMB
A Sumerian shepherd holds a lamb. Sheep not only provided meat and milk, but the sheepskin garments that were commonly worn. Wool was also woven into cloth to make long tunics, dresses and shawls. People had to pay a proportion of the goods they produced as taxes to the city-states.

FOOD SOURCE
Cows were an important part of the Mesopotamian economy. Many different kinds of cheese and other dairy products are mentioned in clay tablet records. One Sumerian temple frieze shows work in a dairy, with two men churning butter in large jars. Other men are straining a substance from one vessel to another to make cheese.

WATER LIFELINE
Summers in Mesopotamia were very hot and dry. From the earliest settlements in Sumer to present-day Iraq, farmers have dug channels to carry water from the Tigris and Euphrates rivers to their fields. Mesopotamian kings believed that organizing the building of canals was a religious duty.

MAKE A RAM-HEADED DRINKING CUP
You will need: paper cup, newspaper, masking tape, scissors, flour and water to make papier mâché, fork, fine sandpaper, paint and paintbrushes, varnish.

1 Scrunch up a piece of newspaper. Attach the ball of newspaper to the bottom end of the paper cup with pieces of masking tape.

2 Make a paste with water and flour using the fork to mix the paste. Tear strips of newspaper and dip them into the paste, then cover the cup.

3 Twist two pieces of newspaper into coil shapes for the horns and attach them to the cup. Cover the cup inside and out with papier mâché. Let dry.

A Healthy Diet

By looking at ancient seeds, archaeologists have been able to find out what people ate in the past. The Mesopotamians ate fruit and vegetables such as apples, pomegranates, medlars and grapes, onions, leeks and turnips. The country's most important crop was barley, which was used for making bread and beer. Wheat was grown to a lesser extent. Barley was made into an oatmeal-like mixture flavored with cumin, mustard, cilantro and watercress.

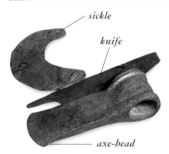

apples

medlars

grapes

pomegranates

Date Orchards

Some of the biggest date orchards in the world are in the south of modern Iraq. The fruits were important in ancient times because they were an excellent source of energy. Dates could be dried and stored so that they were available all year, and were made into wine. Date syrup was used as a sweetener.

Animal-headed cups for drinking wine have been found at Nimrud. Your cup is copied from a pottery one. Wealthy people also used cups of bronze.

sickle

knife

Ancient Tools

Agricultural tools were made of copper and bronze, and included axe-heads, knives and sickles for harvesting. Ancient farmers also had seed drills and wooden plows drawn by oxen, like the ones still used today, although many modern farmers also use tractors.

axe-head

4 When the papier mâché is completely dry, smooth it down with sandpaper. Paint the whole cup in a creamy beige color.

5 When the base coat is dry, use a fine paintbrush and brown paint to add details to your cup. Paint in the ram's horns and face.

6 Use red paint to add stripes to your drinking cup. Paint three red stripes around the neck, and two red stripes around the open end.

7 When the paint is completely dry, coat the drinking cup with a water-based varnish. Allow the first coat to dry before applying a second coat.

31

Science and Technology

THE PEOPLE OF MESOPOTAMIA developed many different aspects of technology including metalworking, pottery, glassmaking, the manufacture of textiles and leather-working. They were also experts at irrigation and flood control, building elaborate canals, water storage and drainage systems. They were among the first people in the world to use metal. An early copper sculpture, made in 2600 B.C., comes from the temple of Ubaid near Ur. It shows a lion-headed eagle clutching two stags in its talons. The armies used vast amounts of bronze for their weapons and armor. King Sennacherib used striding lions, cast in solid bronze and weighing hundreds of kilograms, to support the wooden pillars of his palace at Nineveh.

SUPPLYING THE CITY
Water wheels and aqueducts such as these are still used in the Middle East today. The Assyrians built aqueducts to take water to the cities to meet the needs of their growing populations. The Assyrian king Sennacherib (701-681 B.C.) had 6 miles of canals cut from the mountains to the city of Nineveh. He built dams and weirs to control the flow of water, and he created an artificial marsh, where he bred wild animals and birds.

A WEIGHTY CHALLENGE
Workers in a quarry near the Assyrian city of Nineveh prepare to move an enormous block of stone roughly hewn in the shape of a lamassu (human-headed winged bull). The stone is on a sleigh carried on wooden rollers. At the back of the sleigh some men have thrown ropes over a giant lever and pull hard. This raises the end of the sleigh and other workers push a wedge underneath. More workers stand ready to haul on ropes at the front of the sleigh. At a signal everyone pulls or pushes and the sleigh moves forward.

MAKE A PAINTED PLATE
You will need: a plate, flour, water and newspaper to make papier mâché, scissors, pencil, fine sandpaper, ruler, paints and paintbrushes.

1 Tear strips of newspaper and dip them in the water. Cover the whole surface of the plate with the wet newspaper strips.

2 Mix up a paste of flour and water. Cover the newspaper strips with the paste. Allow to dry, then add two more layers, let it dry each time.

3 When the papier mâché is dry, trim around the plate to make a neat edge. Remove the plate. Add more papier mâché to strengthen the plate.

MAKING CLOTH

Spinning and weaving were usually done by women in the home or in state or temple factories. Large herds of sheep and goats were kept to produce wool, to make clothing. Flax was grown for its fibers, which were used to make linen as early as 3000BC. Cotton was not introduced until the reign of Sennacherib in the 700s B.C.

sheep's wool

wool

sheep's fleece

METALWORKERS

Ceremonial daggers demonstrate the Sumerians' skill at working with gold. Real weapons would have had bronze blades. The Sumerians cast metal by making a wax model of the object required which they covered with clay to make a mold. A small hole in the side let the wax escape when it was heated, so that molten metal could be poured into the mold. When the metal cooled, the mold was broken and the object removed.

You have copied a plate from Tell Halaf, a small town where some of the finest pots in the ancient world were made. They were decorated with orange and brown paints made from oxides found in clay.

HANDMADE VASES

Vases found in Samarra in the north of Mesopotamia were produced about 6,000 years ago. They were shaped by hand and fired in a kiln, then painted with geometric designs. Later, a wheel like a turntable was used to shape the clay, which speeded up the process.

4 When the papier mâché is completely dry, smooth it down with fine sandpaper. Then paint the plate on both sides with a white base coat.

5 When the paint is dry, use a pencil and ruler to mark a dot in the center of the plate. Draw four large petals around this point and add details as shown above.

6 When you are happy with your design, paint in the patterns using three colors for the basic pattern. Allow each color to dry before adding the next.

7 Add more detail to your plate, using more colors, including wavy lines around the edge. When you have finished painting, let dry.

Travel by Land and Water

TRANSPORTING LOGS
Phoenician ships tow logs of cedar wood along the Mediterranean coast. There was no wood in Assyria that was suitable for the palace roofs, so cedar was imported from Phoenicia. When they reached land, the logs were dragged overland on sleighs. Once they reached the rivers, the timber could be floated again. Heavy goods were also often transported on rafts supported by inflated animal skins.

THE TIGRIS AND EUPHRATES rivers and their tributaries provided a very good communications network around the country, so most people traveled by boat rather than on foot. In the south, boats were made of reeds, and were very convenient for getting around in the marshy areas at the head of the Gulf. Once the wheel had been introduced, some wealthy people traveled by horse and chariot along roads and local tracks. Chariots were mainly used by the Assyrian kings and their courtiers when hunting and in battle. At rivers, the chariots were dismantled and carried across on boats. The soldiers swam across using inflated animal skins as life belts. The horses had to get over as best they could.

BEST FOOT FORWARD
People without transportation had to walk, but everyone traveled by boat or cart whenever possible. Conquered people often traveled hundreds of miles from their original homes to new ones in Assyria and Babylonia. These people have been conquered by the Assyrians, and they are taking heavy bales of woolen cloth as a tribute to their new king. Armies marched vast distances too, wearing high leather boots. King Nebuchadnezzar I of Babylon led his armies on a grueling march to Susa at the height of summer to recapture the statue of Marduk, the chief god of Babylon.

MAKE A BOAT

You will need: cutting board, modeling clay, piece of dowel about 8 in. long, toothpick, paints and paintbrushes, glue, varnish and brush, string, scissors.

1 Make an oval dish shape out of the clay. It should measure 5½ in. long x 4¼ in. wide x 1½ in. deep. Make a mast hole for the dowel and attach it to the base.

2 Trim around the top of the boat to smooth it out. Use the toothpick to make four holes through the sides. Let the boat dry out completely.

3 Paint the boat all over with a light brown base color. Then using a brush and your finger, flick contrast colors to create a mottled effect.

Seafaring Nation

The Phoenicians of the eastern Mediterranean, whose cities were conquered by the Assyrian kings, were the great sailors and shipbuilders of the time. They traded fine ivory and metal work, and richly colored woolen cloth, throughout the Mediterranean and beyond. The ships were large and many-oared, and the sailors worked out how to navigate by the stars. The Phoenicians may have been the first people to sail around Africa—via the Strait of Gibraltar, the southern tip of Africa, and along the east coast to the Red Sea.

Small boats are still used today on the River Euphrates. Your boat is based on a model clay boat from 4000 B.C. It has a mast for a light sail. It might have been steered using oars or a punt pole.

Overland Excursions

By about 900 B.C., spoked wheels had replaced the earlier wheels made from a single piece of solid wood. In Sumerian times, onegars (wild asses) hauled chariots, while oxen and mules were used for heavy goods. Traders carried their goods on long caravans (lines) of donkeys that were sturdy enough to travel long distances. From about 900 B.C. the Assyrians used camels as well. Local roads were little more than tracks, but messengers and state officials sped on horseback along the well-maintained roads between the main centers of the Assyrian Empire.

4 Put a drop of glue inside the mast hole. Put more glue around the end of the dowel and push it into the hole. This is your mast.

5 Wait until the glue has dried and the mast is firm. Then paint a layer of water-based varnish all over the boat. Let dry and repeat.

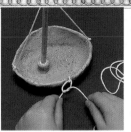

6 Take two lengths of string about 23½ in. long. Tie the end of one piece through one of the holes, around the top of the mast and into the opposite hole.

7 Complete the rigging of the boat by tying the other piece of string through the empty holes and around the top of the mast as before. Trim the strings.

Banking and Trade

TROPHIES AND TAX
Carved ivory furniture, like this panel, and bronze bowls were often carried off after successful battles. There is little evidence of trade in Mesopotamia from 900 to 600 B.C. The Assyrian kings took anything they wanted from the people they defeated. They collected as tax whatever was needed, such as straw and food for horses.

TRADE TO KANESH
Donkeys or mules are still used to transport goods from one village to another in modern Iraq. When trade with ancient Turkey was at its peak, donkey caravans (lines) took large amounts of tin and textiles through the mountain passes to Kanesh. A typical load for one donkey would usually consist of 130 minas (about 145 pounds) of tin (which was specially packed and sealed by the city authorities), and ten pieces of woolen cloth.

THE PEOPLE OF MESOPOTAMIA were very enterprising and expert business people. They traveled long distances to obtain goods they needed, importing timber, metal and semiprecious stones.

Around 2000 B.C., the Assyrians had a widespread, long-distance trading network in Anatolia (modern Turkey). The headquarters were in the northern Mesopotamian city of Ashur and the trade was controlled by the city government and by large family firms.

The head of a firm usually stayed in Ashur but trusted members of the family were based in Anatolian cities such as Kanesh. From here they conducted business on the firm's behalf, going on business trips around Anatolia, and collecting any debts or interest on loans. Deals were made on a credit basis, for the Assyrian families acted as money-lenders and bankers as well. On delivery, goods and transportation (the donkeys) were exchanged for silver, which was then sent back to Ashur. In about 2000 B.C., one Kanesh businessman failed to send back the silver, and the firm threatened to send for the police.

PRECIOUS THINGS

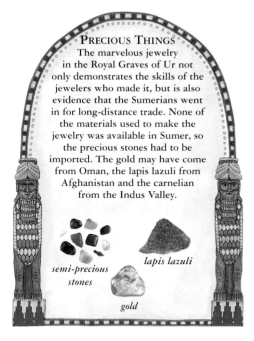

The marvelous jewelry in the Royal Graves of Ur not only demonstrates the skills of the jewelers who made it, but is also evidence that the Sumerians went in for long-distance trade. None of the materials used to make the jewelry was available in Sumer, so the precious stones had to be imported. The gold may have come from Oman, the lapis lazuli from Afghanistan and the carnelian from the Indus Valley.

semi-precious stones

lapis lazuli

gold

STRIKING A DEAL

Two merchants make a contract. One is agreeing to supply goods for a certain amount of silver, and the other is promising to pay by a certain date. The details of a deal were written on a clay tablet and impressed with the cylinder seals of the two men. Often a copy was made and put in a clay envelope. If there was a dispute about the deal later, the envelope would be broken and the agreement checked.

LETTERS FROM KANESH

The site of the trading settlement of Kanesh, where the Assyrians did an enormous amount of business, has been excavated. A great many clay tablets were found, many of them business letters. From these letters, it is clear that the Anatolian princes had the first pick of the goods brought by Assyrian merchants. They charged the merchants taxes on their donkey caravans. In return, the princes protected the roads and provided insurance against robbers.

CASH AND CARRY

There was no money in Mesopotamia, so goods were usually paid for in silver. Silver was measured in shekels and each shekel weighed about ¼ ounce. It was carefully weighed to make sure that the person paying gave an amount equal to the value of the goods bought.

An Important City

THE CITY OF ASHUR was where the country of Assyria began, in the third millennium B.C. When the Assyrian Empire grew vast and mighty, the province of Ashur was called 'The Land,' because it was the original land of Assyria.

By around 2000 B.C., Ashur was a flourishing business center, the focus of the wealthy trade with Anatolia. The City Council, which included the heads of important local families, controlled trade and was very powerful. Although the king was the leading member of the Council, he had to take the Council's advice. In later times, kings had greater power, but the Council still retained some special privileges. As time went on, Ashur became the capital of a growing state, and several kings built temples and palaces there. During the Assyrian Empire, Nimrud or Nineveh became the capital cities, but Ashur remained both the chief religious center, the home of the god Ashur, and the place where Assyrian kings were crowned and buried.

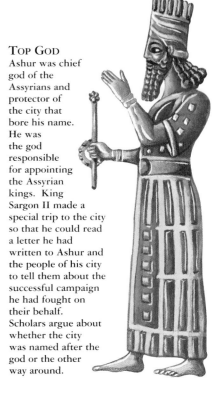

TOP GOD
Ashur was chief god of the Assyrians and protector of the city that bore his name. He was the god responsible for appointing the Assyrian kings. King Sargon II made a special trip to the city so that he could read a letter he had written to Ashur and the people of his city to tell them about the successful campaign he had fought on their behalf. Scholars argue about whether the city was named after the god or the other way around.

DEFENSIVE POSITION
Only traces of the many temples and palaces of Assyria's greatest city can be seen today. The city was built on this rocky spur, above the River Tigris. It was protected by the river on one side and a canal on the other, while steep cliffs enclosed the town to the north and east. The remains of what was once the most impressive building, the ziggurat of Ashur, the city's chief god, are visible on the skyline.

CITY SCENE

This painting shows what the city of Ashur might have been like at its peak. It is based on a painting done by Walter Andrae, the German archaeologist in charge of excavations there in the early 1900s. Although there was no longer much to see above ground, Andrae had uncovered the foundations of so many temples and palaces that he felt he had a very good idea of what the city had been like.

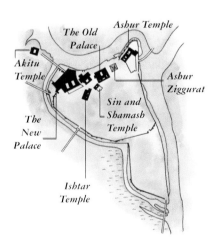

CITY PLAN

Ashur was built high on a rocky outcrop above the River Tigris. To the north and east, the city was protected from attack by steep cliffs. There were temples to the goddess Ishtar and to Sin, the moon god, and Shamash, the sun god. The main temple to the city's god, Ashur, was built in the northeast. The Akitu Temple where the New Year Festival was held lay outside the city walls.

HOME OF THE GODDESS

A statue of Ishtar, goddess of love and war, stands in a niche in her temple. Her temple is made of mud-brick and is the oldest in Ashur. It was begun in about 2500 B.C. and rebuilt seven times. In one of the lowest levels, the archaeologist Walter Andrae found the remains of this cult room, where the goddess was worshiped. Priests and priestesses conducted rituals every day. Along the sides of the room, there were benches where Assyrian people placed statues of themselves, so that they could be seen in a constant act of worship and gain Ishtar's blessing. In the central area were offering tables where food could be left for the goddess. This area also contained copper braziers for burning incense and pottery altars in the shapes of houses.

Running the Empire

FROM THE BEGINNING of the 800s B.C., the country of Assyria began to grow into a vast empire. The land was divided into provinces, each one named after its main city, such as Nineveh, Samaria, Damascus, or Arpad, each with its own governor. The governor had to make sure that taxes were collected, call up soldiers in times of war, and supply workers when a new palace or temple was to be built. He had to provide safe passage for merchants and was responsible for law and order. If the king and his army passed through the province, the governor supplied them with food and drink. A vast system of roads connected the king's palace with governors' residences and all the important cities of the Empire.

ENFORCED REMOVAL
Conquered people are banished from their homeland to go and live in Assyria. These people were from Lachish, near Jerusalem, and were moved to the Assyrian city of Nineveh. The men were used as forced labor in the limestone quarries.

THE KING'S MEN
A king was constantly surrounded by bodyguards, astrologers and other members of the court including provincial governors who helped him run the empire. His attendants included scribes to write down his orders, messengers to deliver them and an attendant to hold a parasol and shield him from the sun. King Ashurnasirpal is celebrating a successful bull hunt with priests and musicians.

MAKE A PARASOL

You will need: pencil, colored card stock 23½ in. x 23½ in, scissors, masking tape, paints in bright colors and paintbrushes, white card stock, string or twine, glue, dowel.

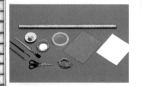

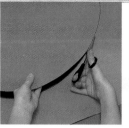

1 Draw a circle on the colored card stock measuring roughly 23½ in. across. Cut out the circle with the scissors keeping the edge as neat as possible.

2 Cut a slit from the edge of the circle to the center. Pull one edge of the slit over the other to make a conical shape. Secure with masking tape.

3 Paint your parasol with red paint. Let dry. Then paint stripes in lots of different shades of orange and red from the top to the bottom.

TOWARD A NEW LIFE

Defeated people camp out en route to a new life in Assyria. The Assyrian Empire grew so big, that it could take months to travel back from a newly conquered territory. People were usually kept together in families and given homes in the countryside. Often they were set to work to cultivate more land.

KEEPING ACCOUNTS

Assyrian scribes at the governor's palace at Til Barsip on the River Euphrates make a note of taxes demanded by the king. Taxes were exacted not only from the local Assyrian people, but also from the conquered territories. They could be paid in produce, such as grain, horses or cattle, and wine.

Kings were accompanied by an attendant carrying a sunshade, which was probably made of fine woolen material and decorated with tassels.

USEFUL TRIBUTE

Horses are given as tributes to the Assyrian king from a conquered people. They will be used to swell the chariot and cavalry units in the Assyrian army. The best-bred and strongest horses came from the foothills of the Zagros Mountains to the east of Assyria. The king also demanded food for the horses.

4 Cut 20 oval shapes about 2 in. x 1½ in. from the white card stock. Cover with a base color of gold. Let dry, then paint with bright designs.

5 Use the scissors to make holes around the edge of the parasol and in the ovals. Attach the ovals to the parasol with twine, knotting it as shown.

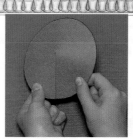

6 Cut a small circle out of colored card stock measuring 4 in. across. Make a slit to the center, and pull one edge over the other as before. Paint the small cone gold.

7 Glue it to the top of the parasol. Paint the handle with gold paint and allow to dry. Attach it to the inside of the parasol using plenty of masking tape.

41

Fighting Forces

WHEELED ADVANTAGE
An Assyrian king charges along in his chariot at a lion hunt. Chariots were also used to ride into battle. The Assyrians perfected the art of chariot warfare, which gave them a big advantage over enemies who were fighting on foot.

THE EARLIEST HISTORICAL RECORDS of Mesopotamia tell of city-states at war with one another. These were usually local disputes over pieces of land or the ownership of canals. Later, when powerful kings created empires, they went to war with foreign countries. King Sargon of Agade, for example, subdued all the cities of Sumer and then went on to conquer the great cities of Mari on the River Euphrates and Ebla in northern Syria. Assyria and Babylonia were often at war in the first millennium B.C. The walls of Assyrian palaces are decorated with reliefs showing frightened groups of Babylonians hiding among the reeds of the marshes, as well as the conquest of Elam, Judah and Phoenician cities.

IN THE BEGINNING
A model of a very early chariot, about 4,000 years old, shows the first wheel designs of solid wood. By the time of the Assyrian Empire, about 900-600 B.C., war chariots had spoked wooden wheels with metal rims.

THE KING'S GUARDS
A panel from the palace of the Persian kings at Susa shows a long procession of king's guards. The guards are armed with spears, and carry quivers full of arrows. King Cyrus of Persia conquered Babylon in 539 B.C.

MAKE A CHARIOT
You will need: pen, cardboard, scissors, paints and paintbrushes, flour, water and newspaper to make papier mâché, glue, masking tape, 2 x dowel 6¼ in. long, cardboard tubes, needle, 4 toothpicks.

1 Cut four circles about 2¾ in. in width out of the cardboard. Use the scissors to make a hole in the center of each circle. Enlarge the holes with a pen.

2 Cut out two sides for the chariot 4¾ in. long x 3 in. high as shown, one back 3½ in. x 3 in., one front 3½ in. x 6 in., one top 3½ in. x 2¾ in. and one base 4¾ in. x 3½ in.

3 Trim the top of the front to two curves as shown. Stick the side pieces to the front and back using masking tape. Stick on the base and top.

SLINGS AND ARROWS

Assyrian foot soldiers used rope slings and stone balls the size of modern tennis-balls. Others fired arrows while sheltering behind tall wicker shields. They wore helmets of bronze or iron and were protected by metal scale armor and leather boots.

GOING INTO BATTLE

Sumerian chariot drivers charge into battle. A soldier armed with spears stands on the foot plate of each chariot ready to jump off and fight. They are all protected by thick leather cloaks and helmets. The chariots were drawn by onegars (wild asses).

Your chariot copies a clay model made in northern Mesopotamia over 4,000 years ago.

STORMING A CITY

Many Assyrian fighting methods can be seen in the palace reliefs at the city of Nimrud. In this scene, the Assyrians storm an enemy city which stands on a hill. A siege engine with spears projecting from the front breaks down the walls. Attacking soldiers would also scale the walls with the help of siege ladders, protected by archers.

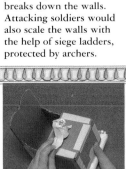

4 Roll up a piece of newspaper to make a cylinder shape 1 in. long, and attach it to the chariot. Attach the cardboard tubes to the bottom of the chariot.

5 Mix a paste of flour and water. Dip newspaper strips into the paste to make papier mâché. Cover the chariot with layers of papier mâché. Let dry.

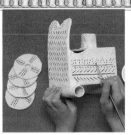

6 Paint the whole chariot cream. Add detail using brown paint. Paint the wheels, too. Make a hole with the needle in each end of the dowels.

7 Insert a toothpick in the dowel, add a wheel and insert into the tube. Attach another wheel and stick to the other end. Repeat with the other wheels.

Palace Builders

A MESOPOTAMIAN PALACE was not just built as the king's residence but also as a center of government. Many were impressive buildings where the kings received ambassadors.

Most information about palace buildings comes from the Assyrian palaces at Nimrud, Nineveh and Khorsabad. King Ashurnasirpal built a magnificent palace at Nimrud on the River Tigris in the 900s B.C. He knocked down the old city and built a huge platform of 120 layers of mud-bricks as a foundation. On that platform, he wrote, 'I built my palace with seven beautiful halls roofed with boxwood, cedar, cypress and terebinth wood. I decorated the doors with bands of bronze. I carved and painted the walls with vivid paint showing my victories.' The king had lapis lazuli colored glazed bricks specially made and set them in the walls above the gates.

HAULING WOOD
Workers drag heavy pieces of cedar wood to the building site of the palace at Nimrud. The timber for the palace roof and the imposing doors at the entrance was imported from Lebanon, which was famous for its pine and cedar wood. It came by boat along the Mediterranean coast. Once the ships were unloaded, the timber was hauled overland to the city.

MIGHTY BEASTS
Lamassus were huge statues that stood at palace entrances to frighten evil spirits away from the palace and the king. They were carved from a single block of gypsum, a soft stone that was easy to carve, and weighed several tons. They have five limbs so that they have four legs when seen from the side. The extra leg was so that they did not appear one-legged if seen from the front.

EXOTIC SETTING
Assyrian palaces were often set in exotic gardens. At Nimrud in 970 B.C., King Ashurnasirpal took pride in his garden where he planted all kinds of seeds and plants brought back from his campaigns in foreign countries. He had vines, nut trees and fruit trees. He wrote: 'Pomegranates glow in my garden of happiness like stars in the sky. In my garden the plants vie with each other in fragrance. The paths are well kept and there are canals so the plants can be watered.'

YOU HAVE BEEN WARNED

Palace walls were decorated with carved reliefs designed to impress visitors, and to show that the king was fulfilling the role given to him by the gods. In this relief at Ashurnasirpal's palace at Nimrud, the king is depicted heroically fighting a snarling lion, proving that he is the protector of his people. Other scenes showed the king victorious in battle, as a warning to anyone considering rebellion against Assyria.

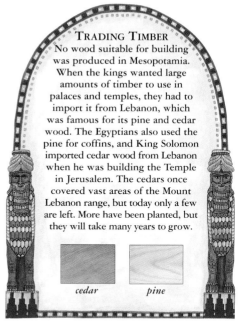

TRADING TIMBER

No wood suitable for building was produced in Mesopotamia. When the kings wanted large amounts of timber to use in palaces and temples, they had to import it from Lebanon, which was famous for its pine and cedar wood. The Egyptians also used the pine for coffins, and King Solomon imported cedar wood from Lebanon when he was building the Temple in Jerusalem. The cedars once covered vast areas of the Mount Lebanon range, but today only a few are left. More have been planted, but they will take many years to grow.

cedar   pine

WEALTH AND SPLENDOR

Henry Layard, the archaeologist who excavated the city of Nimrud in the 1840s, imagined the city looked like this at the height of its powers. His picture was based on his excavations, but it may not be entirely accurate. However, it gives an idea of the splendor and wealth of an Assyrian capital city. Archaeologists found the remains of several palaces and temples at Nimrud. They had been built by various kings in the 8th and 9th centuries B.C.

Furnishing the Palace

WOMAN IN A WINDOW
The Phoenicians were very skillful at ivory carving. This piece, showing a woman looking out of a window, is typical of their work. The holes were used to attach it to a mirror handle.

THE ASSYRIAN KINGS loved the luxury of ivory furniture. They filled their palaces with ivory beds, armchairs, footstools and tables. No complete pieces of ivory furniture have survived to modern times, but Henry Layard found part of an ivory throne at Nimrud in the 1840s. He also found some whole tusks of elephant ivory and a great many small, carved ivory plaques that were once attached to the wooden framework of pieces of furniture. The Assyrians were free to use as much ivory as they liked because elephants were not then an endangered species. No textiles have survived but palaces would probably have been made more comfortable with cushions and woolen rugs. Stone entrances to the palace rooms carved in the form of floral-patterned carpets show us what the rugs may have looked like.

INSIDE THE PALACE
Palaces were built from mud-brick, but the lower interior walls were decorated with carved and painted slabs of stone. Teams of sculptors and artists produced scenes showing the king's military campaigns and wild bull and lion hunts. The upper walls were plastered and painted with similar scenes to glorify the king and impress foreign visitors. Paints were ground from minerals. Red and brown paints were made from ochers, blues and greens from copper ores, azurite and malachite.

MAKE A BRONZE AND IVORY MIRROR

You will need: pencil, thick white and reflective (silver) card stock, ruler, scissors, thick dowel, masking tape, flour, water and newspaper for papier mâché, sandpaper, paints and brushes, glue.

1 Using a pencil, draw a circle 4¾ in. across onto the strong white card stock. Add a handle about 2¼ in. long and 1 in. wide as shown. Cut out.

2 Take a length of dowel about 8 in. long. Attach the dowel to the handle using masking tape. Bend the card stock around the dowel as shown in the picture.

3 Scrunch up a piece of newspaper into a ball. Attach the newspaper ball to the top of the handle with masking tape as shown.

LUXURY IN THE GARDEN

King Ashurbanipal and his wife even had luxurious ivory furniture in the palace gardens at Nineveh. In this picture, the king is reclining on an elaborate ivory couch decorated with tiny carved and gilded lions. The queen is sitting on an ivory chair with a high back and resting her feet on a footstool. Cushions make the furniture more comfortable. Ivory workers used drills and chisels similar to those used by carpenters. The ivory plaques had signs on them to show how they should be slotted together.

SOURCES OF IVORY

Ivory furniture came from Phoenicia as booty. The Phoenicians had two main sources of elephant ivory. From the 15th to the 9th centuries B.C. there were elephants in nearby Syria, although they do not live there today. This would have been their nearest source. The Phoenicians were great sailors and often went to Egypt where they may well have traded some of their goods for ivory that had come from Africa.

ivory

African elephant

Polished bronze was used for mirrors in ancient times. A mirror with a carved ivory handle would have belonged to a wealthy woman.

BOY-EATER

This furniture plaque shows a boy being eaten by a lioness. The boy's kilt is covered with gold leaf, and his curly hair is made of tiny gold pins. There are lotus flowers and papyrus plants in the background, inlaid with real lapis lazuli and carnelian. Sometimes ivory was stained or inlaid with paste to imitate jewels.

4 Make a paste with flour and water, and dip strips of newspaper in it. Cover the handle with several layers, allowing each layer to dry.

5 Use newspaper to make the nose and ears. Add a strip of papier mâché at the top of the head for the crown. Let dry, then sandpaper until smooth.

6 Paint a base coat of gray paint on the face and bronze on the handle. Then add the details of the face and crown in black using a fine paintbrush.

7 Cut out a circle of reflective card stock to match the mirror shape. Glue the reflective card stock carefully onto the white card stock. This is your bronze mirror.

Marvellous Sculptures

PROTECTIVE GENIE
Many rooms in the palace King Ashurnasirpal built at Nimrud in the 900s B.C. were decorated with genies. These creatures have human bodies but the wings, heads and beaks of birds of prey. They were carved to protect the king and the courtiers from evil spirits. The genie shown here is carrying a cone and a bucket and seems to be using them for some kind of ritual. He was possibly blessing the king.

FROM THE BEGINNING of the civilization in Mesopotamia, sculpture was an important art. The earliest sculptors were good at making small statues and figurines. Some were made of stone, but others were of painted clay. Apart from boulders found in rivers there was no stone in Sumer, so most of the materials for sculpture had to be imported. In Assyria, further north, there were quarries near the modern town of Mosul, where a kind of gypsum was found. This is a fairly soft stone which can be carved in great detail. Large pieces of gypsum were cut with pickaxes and sawed with two-handled saws. The slabs were then put on carts and taken to the river where they were transferred onto rafts and floated to the building site. The slabs were carved and painted after they were placed in position.

OFF TO WORK
Men go to work at a gypsum quarry near to the modern city of Mosul on the River Tigris. It was not far from the ancient Assyrian cities of Nimrud and Nineveh. The workers are carrying pickaxes to hack out massive blocks of stone. The two-handled saws will be used to slice the blocks into thinner slabs to be attached to the walls of a palace before they are carved and painted by teams of artists.

GLAZED BRICKS FROM BABYLON
Babylonian kings decorated their city with beautiful sculptures made of glazed bricks. This panel comes from the Ishtar Gate at Babylon. It shows the mushushshu (snake dragon) of the city god Marduk. The gate also featured bulls. The animals were made from glazed bricks formed in special molds so that they stood out from the wall as if they had been carved.

CHOSEN BY ASHUR

In this carved relief from the throne room in Ashurnasirpal's palace, the king is shown twice. He is standing in front of a sacred tree. Above the tree is a winged disc containing the figure of a god. He seems to be pointing at Ashurnasirpal to indicate he is the god's choice. The god could be Ashur.

MONSTER GUARDIAN

Assyrian palace entrances were guarded by lamassus, immense statues three metres high or more. When a sculpture was complete, it was painted to make it more lifelike. Lamassus were strange monsters with the bodies of lions or bulls, the wings of mighty birds, human heads and caps with horns to show they had divine powers. They combined all the most powerful forces of heaven and earth and were supposed to prowl up and down warding off evil spirits from the palaces. They are symbols of pent-up supernatural fury.

PUBLIC DISPLAY

Assyrian kings liked to be seen as faithful servants of the gods. They often ordered a stela (stone slab) to be set up in a public place and carved with pictures. This stela was set up outside the temple of Ninurta, the war god, at Nimrud. It shows King Ashurnasirpal showing respect to the gods. The symbols represent different gods—the goddess Ishtar (star), Adad the storm god (forked lightning), Sin the moon god (crescent Moon), Shamash the sun god (disc with flames), and Ashur (horned cap).

RELIEF WORK

Stone was cut into large slabs at the quarry site using tough, two-handled saws. The slabs were taken to the palace or temple. Workers joined them together by hammering lead dowels and clamps into them with mallets. Then teams of sculptors would carve the figures in outline with big bronze or iron chisels, and then use finer ones for details of face, hair, jewelry and dress. The carved surface was then polished with sand or painted.

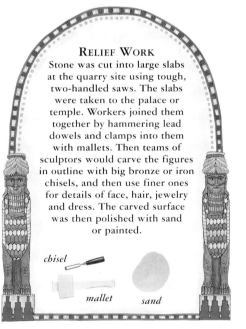

chisel

mallet

sand

The Lion Hunt of the King

FROM EARLIEST TIMES, Mesopotamian kings hunted lions, because lions represented evil and it was the duty of the king to protect his people. The first known picture of a king doing this is on a stela (stone slab) from the ancient Sumerian city of Uruk and is over 5,000 years old. Most of our information about royal lion hunts comes from reliefs in a sloping corridor of the palace of the Assyrian king Ashurbanipal (669-631 B.C.) at Nineveh, which show every stage of a hunt. When the lion had been killed, the king poured a libation of oil or wine over the body, and offered it to the gods.

AFRICAN LION
Mesopotamian mountain lions were smaller than the African lion shown here but were just as dangerous. They came from the mountains and attacked the villagers of the plain and their farm animals. The mountain lions are extinct now but lived in Mesopotamia until the 1800s.

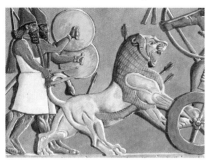

LION ARENA
A hungry snarling lion has been released from its cage. The kings did not hunt lions in open country but in special arenas heavily guarded by soldiers, gamekeepers and fierce dogs. The royal hunting ground was just outside Nineveh, and lions were brought there in strong cages. Local people sometimes climbed nearby hills to get a good view.

HUNTING FOR FOOD
The Mesopotamians were good farmers, growing barley and other crops and raising sheep and goats, but they also had to go hunting for meat to supplement their diet. These men have shot a deer using a bow and arrow and trapped a rabbit in a snare. Sometimes, they caught birds using nets, and they collected locusts. Marsh scenes carved on the palace walls show men and boys fishing from boats or sitting on inflated animal skins.

MAKE A ROYAL TUNIC
You will need: coloured cotton fabric 35 in. x 90½ in., white pencil, tape measure, scissors, pins, needle and thread, white cotton fabric 19½ in. x 9½ in., pencil, fabric paints and paintbrushes, glue, sponge.

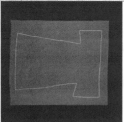

1 Fold the colored cloth in two. Using the white pencil, draw a tunic shape as shown. It should be roughly 35 in. across and 45 in. long.

2 Cut out the tunic shape, making sure that you are cutting through both layers of material. Be careful to cut the lines as smoothly as you can.

3 Pin around the edges of the two tunic shapes. Then sew down the sides and across the top, making sure you leave holes for your head and arms.

PROTECTOR OF THE PEOPLE

Hunters were heavily armed. Here King Ashurbanipal's arrows have only injured the lion. When the lion attacks his horse, the king plunges his spear into it. Eventually, the lion is worn out, and the king dismounts and thrusts his sword into the lion. Because the lion symbolized evil to the Mesopotamians, the king is not just hunting for sport. It is the king's religious duty to protect his people from such evil.

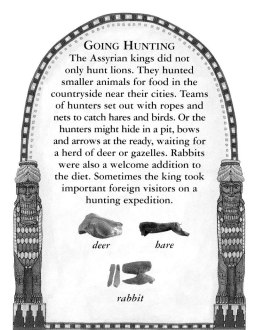

GOING HUNTING

The Assyrian kings did not only hunt lions. They hunted smaller animals for food in the countryside near their cities. Teams of hunters set out with ropes and nets to catch hares and birds. Or the hunters might hide in a pit, bows and arrows at the ready, waiting for a herd of deer or gazelles. Rabbits were also a welcome addition to the diet. Sometimes the king took important foreign visitors on a hunting expedition.

deer   *hare*

rabbit

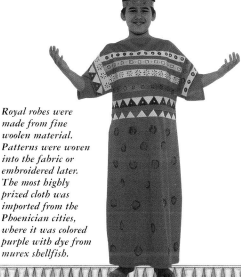

Royal robes were made from fine woolen material. Patterns were woven into the fabric or embroidered later. The most highly prized cloth was imported from the Phoenician cities, where it was colored purple with dye from murex shellfish.

4 Neaten the edges of the arms and around the bottom by turning in a small amount of material to make a hem. Pin the hem, then sew it as shown.

5 Draw strips about 1 in. wide on the white material. Paint brightly colored decorative designs along the strips with the fabric paints.

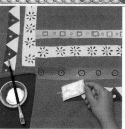

6 When the paint is dry, cut out the decorative strips, keeping the lines as straight as you can. Glue the strips on to the tunic across the chest and arms.

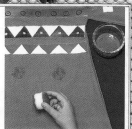

7 Use the sponge to make decorative patterns on the rest of the tunic. Dip the sponge into fabric paint and press it lightly onto the fabric.

Kingship

THE KINGS OF MESOPOTAMIA considered themselves to have been chosen by the gods. For example, Ur-Nanshe of Lagash (2480 B.C.) said that he was granted kingship by Enlil, chief of the gods, and Ashurbanipal (669 B.C.) claimed he was the son of the Assyrian god, Ashur, and his wife, Belit. The Mesopotamian kings ran the state on the god's behalf. Even in the Assyrian Empire, when the kings had grand titles such as 'King of the Universe,' they still felt they were responsible to the gods for the well-being of their people. Another of their titles was 'Shepherd.' This meant they had to look after their people, just as a shepherd tends his flock.

AUTHORITY
This onyx mace belonged to the Babylonian kings. It was a symbol of authority. At the New Year festival, the king placed his mace before the statue of the chief god, Marduk. He was later given back the mace so that he could reign for another year.

SUN GOD TABLET FROM SIPPAR
Kings had to see that temples and statues of the gods were kept in good repair. This tablet shows King Nabu-apla-iddina of Babylon being led into the presence of the god Shamash. The story on the tablet tells us that the king wanted to make a new statue of the god. He was meant to repair the old one but it had been stolen by enemies. Fortunately a priest found a model of the statue that could be copied.

MAKE A FLY WHISK

You will need: calico fabric, pencil, ruler, white glue and brush, scissors, thick card stock, paints and paintbrushes, newspaper.

1 Draw long leaf shapes about 17¾ in. long onto the calico fabric with the pencil. Paint the shapes with watered down white glue. Let dry.

2 Cut out the leaf shapes. Make a card spine for the center of each leaf as shown, thicker at the bottom than at the top, and glue them on.

3 Paint the leaves in gold, yellow and red paints on both sides. Add fine detail by cutting into the edge of each leaf using the scissors.

FIGHTING FOR THE GODS

Kings believed that they were commanded by the gods to conquer in their name. In this relief, King Sennacherib is sitting on his throne receiving the booty and prisoners taken after the city of Lachish had fallen. The king devoted a whole room in his palace at Nineveh to the story of this siege. He also made war on Babylon and completely devastated the city. In 612 B.C. the Babylonians had their revenge. They destroyed Nineveh and hacked out Sennacherib's face on this sculpture.

EXPLORATION AND DISCOVERY

Another mark of good kingship was the expansion of knowledge. King Shalmaneser III sent an expedition to find the source of the River Tigris pictured here. When his men found it, they set up a stela to record the event and made offerings to the gods to celebrate. Many of the Mesopotamian kings were learned men. Kings such as Ashurbanipal collected clay tablets to make great libraries. Others collected exotic plants and animals.

Fly whisks made of long thin leaves or feathery reeds kept the flies away from the king. They could also be used as a fan to keep him cool.

4 Draw two identical handle shapes onto the stiff card stock. They should be about 8½ in. long and 4 in. wide at the top. Cut out the shapes.

5 Tear up newspaper strips and dip into glue. Wrap the strips around the edges of the two handles to fasten them together. Leave the top of the handle unglued.

6 Decorate the handle with gold paint. Let dry. Paint decorative details on to the gold with black paint using a fine paintbrush.

7 Glue the bottoms of the leaves and push them into the top of the handle, between the two pieces of cardboard. Spread the leaves well apart.

53

Royal Libraries and Museums

IN THE MID-700S B.C., King Ashurbanipal decided to found a great library at Nineveh. Every temple in the land had a library, so he sent his scribes round all the temples of Babylonia with instructions to bring him anything that looked interesting. If the priests were reluctant to let a tablet go, the scribes were told to make a copy. The library at Nineveh eventually contained over 25,000 clay tablets, and most of what is known about Mesopotamian learning comes from there.

In the Nineveh library were ancient myths and legends such as the *Epic of Gilgamesh* and the *Birth Legend of Sargon of Agade*, dictionaries, mathematical problems, and texts on astronomy, astrology and medicine. There were collections of clay models of sheep's livers and lists of weather omens for predicting future events. For example, if it was foggy in a particular month, the land was expected to go to ruin.

The Babylonian king, Nebuchadnezzar II, founded a museum, which had statues, a stela of a Mari governor who introduced beekeeping into Mesopotamia, and objects and clay tablets that went back to Sumerian times.

WHAT THE FUTURE HOLDS
Clay models of sheep's livers were used for divining what the future might hold. They were divided into zones with names such as Station, Path, Finger and Palace Gates. The diviners used these to interpret what they saw in the livers of sacrificed animals. If the Palace Gates were open, for example, this could mean attack by an enemy, or famine. If they were together, it was a good sign.

WRITING TO GODS
If a king wanted to build a temple or go on a campaign, he asked the gods about it first. The Assyrian king, Esarhaddon, wrote letters to the sun god, Shamash, which were kept in the library at Nineveh. He wrote a question on a clay tablet and asked for a clear answer. The tablet was then placed in front of the god's statue. An animal was slaughtered and the liver examined. The diviners (fortune-tellers) could tell by looking at it whether or not the god approved.

WORK IT OUT
King Ashurbanipal, founder of the library at Nineveh, collected many mathematical tablets. The Babylonians were the world's first mathematicians, and figured out many processes that are still used today. The library had a number of mathematical tables that made it easier for people to divide and multiply numbers. Clay tablets included tables showing reciprocals, square numbers and square roots.

DISCOVERY

Before the discovery of the 4,000-year-old library at Ebla, no one knew that libraries existed at such an early date. The city was mentioned in Sumerian texts but its location was not known. The mound at Tell Mardik in northern Syria was first excavated in the 1960s by Italian archaeologists. Proof that it was the ancient city of Ebla came with the discovery of the royal library, and a royal statue inscribed with the words 'Ibbit-Lim, King of Ebla.'

LOOK IT UP

The oldest library found in the world so far dates from the 3rd millennium B.C. and was discovered at Ebla in north Syria. The city lay beyond Mesopotamia, but the people used similar writing, and kept records just like the Sumerians. This library was found in the palace at Ebla. Tablets were in heaps on the floor, but the excavators could see marks on the walls where shelves had once been. Librarians kept all the tablets about a particular subject together on one part of the shelves. Small tablets were stored in baskets.

MAP OF THE WORLD

A unique map of the world was found in the library of Ashurbanipal at Nineveh, although it was originally drawn up in Babylon. It shows the world as the Babylonians saw it. The earth is a flat disc surrounded by ocean. Babylon is named in the box inside the circle. The River Euphrates flows through the middle. Mysterious regions lie to the north, south, east and west. The north is described as 'the land where the Sun is never seen.' Few people had ever been there, but the text says Sargon of Agade had. He is known from his own records to have conquered distant regions, and was still regarded as a hero hundreds of years later.

Math, Medicine and Astronomy

THE MESOPOTAMIANS liked working things out. They had two number systems, one using 10 as a base and the other, 60. The Sumerians were the first to calculate time in hour-long units of 60 minutes, and their astronomers worked out a calendar based on 12- and 28-day cycles and 7-day weeks from studying the moon and the seasons. In particular, the Babylonians were especially interested in studying the heavens, and their astronomers could predict events like eclipses, solstices and equinoxes.

Mesopotamian doctors did not really understand how the body works, but made lists of patients' symptoms. Their observations were passed on to the Greeks hundreds of years later and so became one of the foundations of modern medicine.

HEAVY COUGH CURE
This tablet suggests mixing balsam (an herb) with strong beer, honey and oil to cure a cough. The mixture was taken hot, without food. Then the patient's throat was tickled with a feather to make him sick. Other prescriptions used mice, dogs' tails and urine.

MEDICINAL BREW
Servants are distilling essence of cedar, a vital ingredient for a headache cure. Cedar twigs were put into a pot, and heated to give off a vapor. It condensed against the cooler lid and trickled into the rim of the pot from where it was collected. The essence was mixed with honey, resin from pine, myrrh and spruce trees, and fat from a sheep's kidney.

BAD OMEN
Eclipses were considered a bad sign. However, an eclipse that was obscured by cloud did not count. When an eclipse could not be seen in a royal city, the king was told it had nothing to do with him or his country and he should not worry about it.

MAKE A SET OF LION WEIGHTS
You will need: pebbles of various sizes, kitchen scales, modeling clay, cutting board, toothpick, paints and paintbrushes.

1 Weigh a pebble and add modeling clay to bring it to a weight of 8 oz. Once the clay has dried out, the final weight will be only about 7 oz.

2 Take a portion of the weighed modeling clay and shape it into a rectangle roughly 4¾ in. x 2¾ in. This will be the base for your weight.

3 Wrap another piece of the weighed modeling clay around the weighed pebble to make the lion's body. Shape the body into a pear shape.

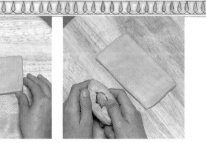

SKY MAP

The sky in this sky map is divided into eight parts and the stars in each section are indicated. The heavens were seen as a source of information about the future, so the kings often consulted astronomers. One astronomer wrote to the king in the 600s B.C.: 'I am always looking at the sky but nothing unusual has appeared above the horizon.'

WEIGHTS AND MEASURES

Officials weigh metal objects that have been taken as booty after a victory. The duck-shaped object is a weight. The kings were responsible for seeing that weights and measures were exact and that nobody cheated customers. Prices were fixed by law and calculated in shekels (1 shekel was about ¼ ounce of silver).

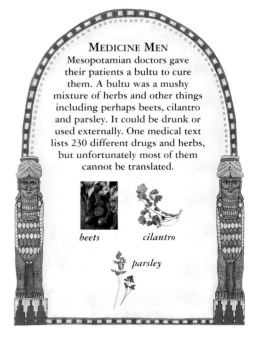

MEDICINE MEN

Mesopotamian doctors gave their patients a bultu to cure them. A bultu was a mushy mixture of herbs and other things including perhaps beets, cilantro and parsley. It could be drunk or used externally. One medical text lists 230 different drugs and herbs, but unfortunately most of them cannot be translated.

beets   *cilantro*

parsley

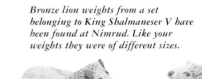

Bronze lion weights from a set belonging to King Shalmaneser V have been found at Nimrud. Like your weights they were of different sizes.

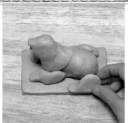

4 Position the pebble and clay onto its base. Add another piece of weighed clay to form the head and mane. Shape the face and jaw with your fingers.

5 Model four pieces of weighed clay to make the lion's four legs and stick them on to the body. Flatten the clay slightly at each end for the paws.

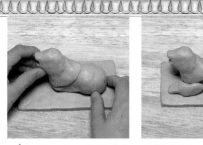

6 Make a tail and ears using up the remaining weighed clay. Using the toothpick, add extra detail to the face, mane, paws and tail. Let dry.

7 Paint the lion and the base cream. Flick with brown paint for a mottled appearance. Add details to the face, mane and paws. Make more lions for a set.

Babylonian Power

ATTACK ON BABYLON
Assyrian kings usually
showed great respect for
Marduk, the god of Babylon.
But when the Babylonians
allowed King Sennacherib's
son to be captured, the
angry king attacked Babylon
and burnt down Marduk's
temple. His son and grandson
were so worried by this that
they decided to rebuild the
city and temple as quickly as
they could. This stela shows
Sennacherib's grandson
Ashurbanipal holding a
brick-basket for building.

REBUILDING BABYLON
Nabopolassar and his son,
Nebuchadnezzar built a new
city worthy of Babylon's status
as a world power in the 500s
B.C. The city was constructed
on both banks of the River
Euphrates with a bridge on
stone pillars connecting the
two parts of the new Babylon.
There were several temples
and palaces. A massive 5-mile
wall surrounded the city. The
road on top of the wall was so
wide that two four-horse
chariots could pass each other.

THE NAME BABYLON means Gateway of the Gods. Although
Babylon was quite a small place in Sumerian times, it began to
grow in importance from the time of King Hammurabi. It soon
became the chief city of the whole of southern Mesopotamia, and this
region became known as Babylonia. The main temple of the god
Marduk was in Babylon, and the city became a great center of learning.
Many of the texts in King Ashurbanipal's library came from Babylonia,
or were copies of Babylonian works. Toward the end of the 600s B.C.,
the Babylonians attacked and destroyed the Assyrian cities of Ashur,
Nimrud and Nineveh. The Assyrian Empire came to an end, and for a
time Babylon became very powerful under its great king,
Nebuchadnezzar II. King Nebuchadnezzar took over many parts of the
ancient world that had once belonged to Assyria, including Palestine
and Phoenicia. When King Necho of Egypt challenged Nebuchadnezzar
and tried to take some of the old Assyrian territory for himself, the
Babylonian king promptly chased him back to his country.

GATEWAY TO THE GODDESS
The inner wall of the city of Babylon had several gateways leading into the city, each having the name of an important god or goddess. The most splendid was the Ishtar Gate, named after the goddess of love and war and built in the reign of Nebuchadnezzar II. The gate was decorated with blue-glazed bricks inset with three-dimensional sculptures of molded bricks. These showed the bull of Adad and the snake dragon of Marduk, the god of Babylon.

A FORMIDABLE ENEMY
King Marduk-apla-iddina was the very first Babylonian king to be mentioned by name in the Bible, where he is called Merodach Baladan. This boundary stone was found in Babylon and shows him making a grant of land to the governor of Babylon in around 700 B.C. Marduk-apla-iddina fought many battles against the Assyrian kings, Sargon and Sennacherib. Even after he had been defeated and forced to retreat to the marshes, he continued to stir up trouble for the Assyrians.

THE WAY OF THE LION
Babylon had a special road for processions. The Processional Way led from the temple of Marduk through the Ishtar Gate on its way out of the city to the temple where the New Year festival was held. The way was decorated with blue-glazed tiles and molded brick figures of lions. Each year the statues of the gods were carried along here to attend a special ceremony in which the Babylonian Story of Creation was enacted and the king was reinstated with royal power.

WONDER OF THE WORLD
The city of Babylon was famous for its Hanging Gardens. Like the pyramids at Giza in ancient Egypt, they were one of the Seven Wonders of the Ancient World. Tradition says the magnificent gardens were created by one of its kings. He had married a Persian wife who was homesick for the hills of her own country. The king loved her so much he built an artificial mountain and planted it with trees and flowers. Later many people tried to find the gardens but no one has ever succeeded, although strangely one modern scholar thinks they were in Nineveh rather than Babylon.

Bible Links

THERE ARE MANY LINKS between Mesopotamia and the Bible. Mesopotamian flood stories are remarkably like the story of Noah's Ark. Abraham, the father of the Israelite and Arab nations, lived at the Sumerian city of Ur before he and his family set off for the Promised Land. Several of the laws and customs relating to marriage and adoption mentioned in these stories about Abraham are like those of Mesopotamia. Jonah was instructed by God to go to the Assyrian city of Nineveh, and the Jewish people were exiled from their Promised Land to Babylon. Assyrian records often include kings and events mentioned in the Old Testament.

One Assyrian king, Shalmaneser III, records his victory at the Battle of Qarqar in Syria. He says that he fought against twelve kings, one of whom was Ahab of Israel. This is the first time a king of Israel appears in the history of another country. From this time onward, the paths of Assyria and Israel often crossed.

FLOODS
A tale like the Bible story of Noah's Ark was found in the library at Nineveh. King Utnapishtim was warned that the god Enlil was going to send a flood and told to make a boat and take his family, all the animals and craftworkers on board. It rained for seven days and seven nights. When it stopped, the king sent out birds to see if the water had gone down. The goddess Ishtar put her necklace in the sky as a sign this would never happen again.

DESERT JOURNEY
Abraham, the father of the Jewish and Arab nations, travels from the Sumerian city of Ur to the country God has promised his people. In this painting of the 1800s, Abraham is leading a wandering existence in a desert landscape with his flock of sheep moving from one area to another in search of grazing ground for his animals. However, people would not have used camels at the time he is thought to have lived, about 2000 B.C. Camels were not used for transport in Mesopotamia until about 1000 B.C.

BLACK OBELISK

The man bowing in front of the Assyrian king, Shalmaneser III, could be Jehu, King of Israel. Israel had been an enemy of Assyria, but Jehu has decided to change sides and become an ally of Assyria. The picture appears on the Black Obelisk, which tells of Shalmaneser III's conquests at war. The writing says that the gifts of the Israelite king are being presented to show his loyalty and win Shalmaneser's approval.

WAR CORRESPONDENTS

The Bible reports that the Assyrian king Sennacherib laid siege to Jerusalem when Hezekiah was king of Judah. It says he withdrew from the siege when an angel attacked his army. In Sennacherib's version of events on this clay prism (a hollow tablet), he does not say he was defeated or that he captured Jerusalem. All he says is he shut Hezekiah up like a bird in a cage.

EXILE IN BABYLON

The great Babylonian king of the 500s B.C. was Nebuchadnezzar II, who took over many parts of the ancient world that had formerly been part of the Assyrian Empire. In 597 B.C. he attacked Jerusalem, the chief city of the kingdom of Judah, a scene imagined here by a medieval painter. At the end of a successful siege, he took the king, his courtiers, the army and all the craftworkers to Babylon. There they spent many years far from home, a time known among Jewish people as the Exile. Nebuchadnezzar took treasures from the temple in Jerusalem as booty. He appointed another king, Zedekiah, to rule in Jerusalem. Nebuchadnezzar returned some years later when Zedekiah rebelled, and punished him severely.

Glossary

A

agriculture Growing crops and breeding animals; farming.

anonymous Without the name of the writer.

archaeologist Someone who studies ancient ruins, tools, coins, seeds, etc. to learn about the past.

astrology The study of the position and movement of the stars and planets in order to foretell the future.

astronomy The scientific study of the stars and planets.

B

banquet A great feast.

booty Valuable things taken away by a victorious army.

C

campaign A series of battles fought by a ruler to bring an area under his control.

cast To shape metal by pouring it into a mold.

city-state A city, its surrounding villages and countryside with its own god and ruler.

civilization A society that is well governed and has made advances in technology and the arts.

civil servant Someone who works for the Government.

cuneiform The wedge-shaped writing invented by the Sumerians and also used by the Babylonians and Assyrians.

D

decipher To work out the meaning of signs and symbols in writing.

deity A god or goddess.

diviner Someone who foretells the future by examining animal's livers or other things such as the pattern oil makes on water.

dynasty A line of rulers all belonging to the same family.

E

empire An area including many different cities and countries and ruled by one person.

epic A long poem about the deeds of a great hero.

equinox In spring and autumn the point when day and night are equal.

excavate To dig in the ground to discover ancient remains.

exploits Great deeds or achievements of kings and heroes.

F

festival A special day set aside to honor a god or goddess.

figurine A small statue.

foundation deposit A group of objects placed in the foundations of a temple by the king who built it.

G

genie A friendly spirit who drives away evil. Statues of genies appear on palace walls blessing the king.

geometric pattern A pattern made by lines, circles and triangles.

glazed bricks Baked bricks, with a colorful, glassy coating.

gypsum A type of limestone used for sculpture quarried near Mosul.

H

hilt Handle of a sword or dagger.

high priest or priestess The chief priest or priestess in a temple who had a special relationship with the deity.

I

impression The shape and pattern left on a clay tablet when a seal is pressed on to it.

inscription Writing done with a reed pen on a clay tablet or with a chisel on stone.

irrigation Bringing water to the fields by using canals and ditches.

ivory Elephant tusks used to make furniture, boxes and handles.

K

knucklebones The small round bones in the feet of animals.

L

lamassu A huge stone statue of a human-headed bull or lion used to guard the entrance to a palace.

lapis lazuli A dark blue, semi-precious stone used for jewelry and seals.

libation A sacrifice of wine or oil poured out in honor of a god or goddess.

lyre A stringed instrument similar to a harp.

M

millennium A span of 1000 years.

mother-of-pearl The inside lining of oyster shells used as inlays for furniture and the frames of musical instruments.

mushushshu A dragon-like creature belonging to Marduk, god of Babylon.

myth A story that seeks to answer a question.

N

nomadic people Those who do not lead a settled life in one place.

O

obelisk A tall, thin, four-sided monument with a stepped top. Used by kings to record their victories.

overlord The ruler of a large state who demands loyalty from a smaller one.

P

prism A hollow, three-dimensional clay tablet with six or eight sides.

province Part of an empire ruled by a governor on behalf of a king.

purification The means by which the king or priest made himself clean so as to be fit to offer sacrifices to his god.

Q

quarry A place where building stone can be dug out of the ground.

R

relief A carved stone slab.

ritual A religious ceremony.

S

sanctuary The most holy place in a temple.

sculpture Carved figures of stone, wood or metal.

semi-legendary Someone who once really lived but about whom fantastic stories are told.

Semitic A family of languages that includes Akkadian, Aramaic and modern Hebrew and Arabic.

solstice Midsummer and midwinter.

stela A large, round-topped piece of stone with the figure of a king and a written account of important events in his reign.

T

tablet A flat piece of clay of varying shape and size used for cuneiform writing.

temple A special building where a god or goddess is worshiped.

terra-cotta Brown-red earthenware used for pots or sculpture.

textiles Fabric or cloth, usually woven from wool, although flax or cotton were sometimes used instead.

treaty An agreement made by cities, countries or kings and vassals.

tribute Payment by a vassal state to his overlord.

U

Underworld The Land of the Dead. The people of Mesopotamia thought it a very gloomy place.

V

vassal The ruler of a small state who acknowledges a greater king as his overlord. He promises to be loyal and pay tribute while his overlord promises to protect him.

vulture A bird of prey often seen on the Assyrian reliefs devouring the bodies of the soldiers who have been killed in battle.

W

warrior A man who fights in wars.

weir A low dam built across a river or canal to control the flow of water.

winged disc A symbol of the sun god Shamash or of Ashur, the chief god of Assyria.

world power A country that becomes one of the most important in the world for a time.

Z

ziggurat A solid, stepped pyramid built of mud-brick with a small temple on top, which is approached by great staircases.

Index